49 WAYS TO PULL
YOURSELF TOGETHER

D1420185

DR. RON IPHOFEN

49 WAYS TO
PULL
YOURSELF TOGETHER

A practical guide to designing and managing your life

DR. RON IPHOFEN FAcSS

First published in Great Britain in 2015 by Step Beach Press Ltd Brighton

A CIP catalogue record for this title is available from the British Library.

ISBN 978-1-908779-39-7

Picture credits: depositphotos.com (photos); freepik.com (illustrations); all other photos © Dr. Ron Iphofen

Series editor: Jan Alcoe

Typeset in Brighton, UK by Step Beach Press Ltd

Printed and bound by Ashford Colour Press Ltd

Step Beach Press Ltd, 28 Osborne Villas, Hove, East Sussex BN3 2RE

www.stepbeachpress.co.uk

49 Ways to Well-being Series

If you have selected this book, you may be looking for practical ways of improving your well-being. If you are a health and well-being practitioner or therapist, you may be helping your clients to improve theirs by encouraging them to practise some of the approaches it is based on. Well-being is a subjective state of 'feeling good' which has physical, mental, emotional and even spiritual dimensions. Because these dimensions overlap and interact, it is possible to improve well-being by making positive changes in any one. For example, taking up regular exercise (a focus on physical well-being) may improve concentration (mental well-being), happiness (emotional well-being) and sense of purpose (spiritual well-being). This series of well-being books is designed to provide a variety of routes to recovering, sustaining, protecting and enhancing well-being, depending on your interests and motivations. While some emphasise psychological techniques, others are based on physical movement, nutrition, journaling and many other approaches.

Each book in the series provides 49 practical ways to improve well-being, based on a particular therapeutic approach and written by an expert in that field. Based on tried and tested approaches from its field, each title offers the user a rich source of tools for well-being. Some of these can be used effectively for improving general resilience, others are especially helpful for particular problems or issues you may be dealing with, for example, recovering from illness, improving relaxation and sleep, or boosting motivation and self-confidence.

Enjoy dipping into any *49 Ways* book and selecting ones which catch your interest or help you to meet a need at a particular time. We have deliberately included many different ideas for practice, knowing that some will be more appropriate at different times, in different situations and with different individuals. You may find certain approaches so helpful or enjoyable that you build them into everyday living, as part of your own well-being strategy.

Having explored one book, you may be interested in using some of the other titles to add to your well-being 'toolbox', learning how to approach your well-being via a number of different therapeutic routes.

For more information about the series, including current and forthcoming titles, visit **www.stepbeachpress.com/well-being**

CONTENTS

A PERSONAL NOTE FROM THE AUTHOR

I will be trying throughout this book to build a personal relationship with you, the unknown reader. It is unusual for a counsellor, coach or mentor to not know much about the one they are advising. So I have had to make some general assumptions about your needs and they have been based on my experiences with other patients, students and friends of mine. But remember there is only one you. There is only one unique being inhabiting your space, your place and your time. So of all the things I suggest I ask only that you try them for yourself, modify them to suit your needs if necessary and continue to seek the solutions for your concerns yourself.

Introduction

WHY THIS BOOK?

In these first few pages I want to convince you that this book is for you. If you've had the curiosity to come this far, pick this book up and read these opening lines, there is already a good chance that this is the book you are looking for. You know that it is said to be a heresy within the 'helping' professions to suggest to someone with a problem to **'pull yourself together'**. Yet in all the books I have ever read about self-improvement and personal development, no one ever does it for you. They all have to get you to do it yourself. What I suggest in this book is that 'pulling yourself together' is the only way you can sort out your problems. In fact, no one else can do it for you.

If you are thinking 'I can't', please don't put this book down just yet. I know from experience that whether you spend years in counselling, visit your therapist regularly, or have a library of self-help books at home, in the last analysis your problems will only be solved when *you* choose to find the way to solve them.

I have come to this conclusion after listening for many years to the experts in the field, listening to my own patients and watching them get better, meeting students of mine after many years and discovering the great achievements that they have accomplished and, yes, reading more books and articles on helping yourself than I can count.

When I say you must pull yourself together I do not suggest that you have to do this alone. Of course, good friends, considerate family and professional experts may all have something to offer you and the growing literature is full of ideas to help you to help yourself. But none of this works unless you make the choice to act upon the advice, to think about the possibilities and to act with concern for your own well-being. In my therapy and teaching I learned long ago that I was only able to help those who wished to help themselves. I could only teach those who wished to learn. It is hard to heal someone who is not also willing to heal themselves.

You can visit counsellors for years and indulge in eternal introspection; some friends and family may enjoy joining in your self-analysis for their own reasons. There are plenty of opportunities for you to be 'listened to' if you look for them or if you are prepared to pay for them. If and when a breakthrough occurs or an insight emerges it will do so because you allowed it and it will only make a difference to your life if you allow it. You must take in what you learn from such moments, remember it and use it – daily. So there is no solution other than *you* taking action, *you* putting in the effort and *you* changing your life for the better. Others will and can help, but only *you* make the difference.

So why choose to read this book from amongst all those available? Because it summarises a wealth of literature and experience, puts it very simply and guides you through the small things that you need to deal with to allow the big things to be confronted. The research for this book draws on the studies in health and motivation I have conducted over many years. It draws on my work as an educator and a therapist for over 40 years. I even coached tennis and squash for several years. I know how to use this knowledge quite directly to get you where you want to be.

Sometimes individuals' own characteristics are obstacles to their own development. At other times it is the systems and structures in which they have to operate that help or hinder the attainment of their goals. Some of the advice contained here helps with dealing with potentially limiting individual characteristics; other advice will show you how to manage limiting or constraining structures. Those structures could be the organisation you work for, or the family system you find yourself in, or the network of friends and associates you are involved with.

But this book also draws on personal experience and my own attempts at pulling *my*self together. Over the years I have experienced many frustrations and things that made me angry, I have suffered from not quite being able to control my environment as I would wish to. All these problems have, at times, brought out the worst in me. So I willingly admit to having made my own mistakes. But there is nothing wrong in that if I am still able to learn from them and, as time goes by, to suffer less from them. I still live in hope they will never occur again. If they do, I draw on a lesson from my coaching days: a good coach does not only instruct and inform, they must be a 'model' too. They must display in their own character and behaviour the very things they are trying to inculcate in their students. One cannot expect students to learn from a coach who can't at least strive to accomplish the things they are asking their students to do. So contained within this book are some of the 'model' ways that I have discovered do actually work and I guarantee that I do apply them myself – every day. Eventually they can become second nature and, without extra thought and effort, they will help you manage your life successfully. This book is about getting you facing in the right direction. Then all you have to do is start walking.

As an intelligent person you already know that there is no perfect solution to all the problems you might have to face in living. There is no ultimate answer and no one right 'way'. What you are doing in reading this book and practising the suggestions made here is working towards a practical response to the world you live in, a *modus vivendi*, a way of living in spite of the lack of the perfect solution. There can be a 'right way' – for *you*. And by reading this book you are already on the way to finding it. What I am presenting you with is a 'plan of action', a programme for designing your life. Please start at the beginning and read each chapter in order and *do* the suggested exercises. Even if you only practise a few of the 'Ways' suggested in what follows, it will make a difference.

Let me explain – the 'logic' of this book

The whole book relates to other books in the *49 Ways* series. Throughout I'll suggest you taking some ideas further by reading other books in the series. But this book is also planned to give you results right away; so there are not a lot of complicated explanations about why a particular suggestion works. I am presenting you with some simple 'tried and true' basic methods that I know do work for people. Try them and use them and judge for yourself. Later you might adjust the ideas to suit your own situation – especially after reading further about them. You will find here quotations from inspirational authors, stories and anecdotes from my own experience and some passed on from others. There are lots of useful suggestions 'out there' to draw upon. Take note of them, even the quotations: allow yourself to stop, think about what they mean and remember them. Most of the ideas you can put into practice on a daily basis, some require a little more patience at first.

For example, the first two chapters are fundamental to laying the foundations for change, so you will need to give them a little more time and thought. **Chapter 1** is designed to start you thinking about yourself in the right way. Perhaps taking on some important new messages and making changes related to your identity: how you see yourself and how others might see you. **Chapter 2** advises about ignoring those voices of doubt that we each have inside our heads that can get in the way of achieving the goals we set ourselves. **Chapter 3** is more practical in offering suggestions about how best to manage your time. **Chapters 4** and **5** are connected in that they are both concerned to help you understand how to harness the power of your own mind and spirit. **Chapter 6** makes some straightforward suggestions about your physical well-being: unless your body is in good order, you won't have the strength to accomplish all the tasks you set yourself.

Chapter 7 does the same with regard to your personal relationships; it is about managing yourself in terms of other people. **Chapters 8** and **9** are connected to designing the 'inner' and the 'outer' you: how best to organise your mind as well as how best to organise your immediate environment. **Chapter 10** is about relationships again, but now that you have your house in order, you can go to a deeper level. You will need to explore the more deeply hidden assumptions you make about yourself and how you deal with others. **Chapter 11** is all about allowing yourself to recognise and take advantage of opportunities. Finally **Chapter 12** offers a way of looking at the whole 'project' of pulling yourself together. Designing your life requires that you have a script or a story that helps you describe exactly where you are going, your aims, goals and how you plan to get there. In some ways this is an overview of all that has gone before. It draws the threads together.

1 2 3 4 5 6 7 8
9 10 11 12 13 14
15 16 17 18 19
20 21 22 23 24
25 26 27 28 29
30 31 32 33 34
35 36 37 38 39
40 41 42 43 44
45 46 47 48 49

Chapter 1

THE IMPORTANCE OF HELPING YOURSELF

'In oneself
lies the whole
world and if
you know how
to look and
learn, then the
door is there
and the key is
in your hand.
Nobody on
earth can give
you either the
key or the door
to open,
except
yourself.'

J. Krishnamurti
You are the World

WAY 1 Taking responsibility

The first step in this programme of action is to examine who *you* are and who you need to be. Give yourself the time to find out who you are.

It is vitally important that you begin by taking responsibility for your own actions. Hold on to a positive view of yourself and never engage in the blame game. Blame neither yourself nor others. Since you are looking for change and improvement you may at present hold a negative perception of yourself. The first step is to learn how to love, admire and appreciate yourself – don't expect or wait for others to do it. So you first need to be responsible for a new, successful identity.

'When you plant lettuce, if it does not grow well, you don't blame the lettuce. You look for reasons it is not doing well. It may need fertilizer, or more water, or less sun. You never blame the lettuce. Yet if we have problems with our friends or family, we blame the other person. But if we know how to take care of them, they will grow well, like the lettuce. Blaming has no positive effect at all, nor does trying to persuade using reason and argument. That is my experience. No blame, reasoning, no argument, just understanding. If you understand, and you show that you understand, you can love, and the situation will change.'
Thich Nhat Hanh

While you must take responsibility, you still have a right to make mistakes. Responsibility and choice lie necessarily with the individual, not with any others or with 'nature'. Nature just 'is'. It holds no feeling or emotions. We human beings do. Start to see the things you do in a positive light. You *can* make mistakes – it is allowed since you are always learning. A mistake is simply another learning experience. That is why there is no blame. Blame stops us allowing for mistakes. It can make us so cautious we don't try anything new. Blaming others for your problems makes you a victim and, therefore, takes power away from you. Blame implies that if someone or something else was at fault then it is not something that we can fix; it leaves us waiting for 'them' to do something about it. It is also why we do not need to blame others – let them try things and make allowances for their mistakes so that they too can learn.

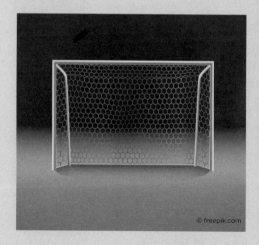

© freepik.com

**'Nihil peccat, nisi quod nihil peccat.'
(He has no faults, except that he has
no faults.)**
Pliny the Younger

Sometimes when you make a mistake your first thought tends to be: 'My plan, my system isn't working. I've put in all this effort and it still doesn't work!' What you forget is that you have been doing well up until the point at which you made the mistake and you perhaps did well because some system or plan of action helped to get you into the correct mental state to do well. But remember that it wasn't 'the system' on its own that produced the successful outcomes (performance or achievement) – it was you who did it! All that is necessary is to allow yourself to get back into the zone of successful accomplishment. Give yourself permission to put the mistake behind you.

As an active agent you are responsible for your own happiness but not for other people's. Others have their own responsibility to take similar actions. Ironically you may be a little fragile and vulnerable to the disenchantment produced by other people. If you have a tender ego, you must keep your new found confidence to yourself. The threat perceived by others to their conventional behaviour and thoughts is best avoided. Your strength will come from having your own secret strategy for success.

Always live in the present, and look to a future of successful outcomes. 'The robbers of time are the past and the future. Man should bless the past and forget it, if it keeps him in bondage, and bless the future, knowing it has in store for him endless joys, but live *fully in the now*.' (Scovel-Shinn 1925: 35)

It is called an 'autosuggestion':

To achieve a particular goal or outcome,
say to yourself over and over (about 20 times):
'... such and such a thing IS going to happen'.

Do not say: 'I will make it happen.'

For example you could say: 'My memory is getting better each day', rather than 'I have an excellent memory.'

Try: 'My new positive identity is emerging day by day.'

Try this

Emile Coué explained how the rational mind gets in the way of accomplishment. It is the unconscious, the imagination, that will achieve the desired outcome as long as we assume its inevitability (Coué 1960: 23). You can commit to your new identity by letting everyone around you know about it; but most importantly you need to commit to it yourself. 'Use your new label to describe yourself every day and it will become conditioned within you' (Robbins 1994: 339).

Most people will say that they just want to be happy. They then try to decide to achieve the things that they think will make them happy. As an example, take a woman who thinks she is not happy but wants to be. She has a great career, lots of friends, travel, money, success. Then she asks herself what is missing since she still isn't happy. Perhaps she decides that she needs a man in her life. So what she thinks is missing is a man; or children or a family or her own home. So she thinks she is not happy because she isn't married. In which case she is *motivated* to find a man because she believes that is what is 'missing' in her life. But the motivation isn't that she needs a man. It's that ... she wants to be happy!

The first step is to decide clearly and uncompromisingly precisely your goal. If it is that you 'want a man in your life' then that's fine – but that is not, in itself, happiness.

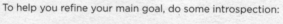

To help you refine your main goal, do some introspection:

Have a blank piece of paper available and a favourite pen.

Start by sitting comfortably and then slowly examine your surroundings in detail.

Where are you sitting? What is the room, the chair, the environment like?

Just observe it first of all.

Then notice yourself: How do you feel?

Are you calm, concerned, interested, excited, confident, optimistic?

Next think about who you are. What sort of person are you?

Think about it for a while and then write down your thoughts. Just make a list: kind, thoughtful, envious, optimistic, pessimistic, hopeful, considerate, worried, attractive, understanding...

Make the list as long as you can then go through it marking with a '+' the characteristics you think of as positive and with a '–' those you think of as negative.

Then ask and answer the question: Who am I?

You may not have an answer that entirely satisfies you at this stage. In fact human beings are remarkably 'fluid' creatures. We can and do change throughout our lives in spite of our belief that we are essentially the 'same person we have always been'. I suggest you do this exercise again when you have finished the book.

'There are times when I look over the various parts of my character with perplexity. I recognise that I am made up of several persons and that the person which at the moment has the upper hand will inevitably give place to another. But which is the real me? All of them or none?'
W. Somerset Maugham

Human experience is incredibly complex. Yet we expect health professionals, for example, to diagnose, prognose, care for and treat the diversity of conditions and people they come across with accuracy and effectiveness. Of course, this is not helped when such professionals themselves assume they can do this without doubt. Or they avoid conveying doubts and uncertainty to the patient in the interests of protecting them. As human beings we manage to 'fool' ourselves in a range of ways; but caring for our own present and future must not be one of them. By taking responsibility for ourselves we will be doing our best to manage the complexity of the human condition. We can choose to seek the help of others, of friends, family or professionals, without passing *all* responsibility over to them, and without expecting too much of them.

This is the beginning of constructing a philosophy of life that will carry you through all situations, no matter how difficult. It is part of establishing your inner core stability. With such a core of stability you are held – physically, emotionally and mentally – and supported throughout all the situations you have to face in your daily life.

'First say to yourself what you would be; and then do what you have to do.'
Epictetus

WAY 2 **Your duty of care**

'On the whole, we are meant to look after ourselves; it is certain each has to eat for himself, digest for himself, and in general care for his own dear life, and see to his own preservation.

Nature's intentions, in most things uncertain, in this are decisive.'
Arthur Hugh Clough

Some people suggest that a concern with one's self is literally rather selfish. They believe that self-help books and manuals don't have a view of how one should be caring for others more and then one would naturally feel better. But doing that might only bury a problem. A very caring or kindly person might be behaving in that way to hide their lack of self-worth or self-esteem and feel that by caring for others they are somehow proving their value. Some people are excessively caring about others to hide the fact that they don't feel good about themselves. Your first duty of care is to your self.

There are some gender differences in taking responsibility for one's self. Women often have the greatest difficulty since they are socialised into caring roles from an early age. They can be led towards being 'responsible' for others; for their happiness, their physical, mental and emotional well-being. Men are more often socialised into taking command, to leading, and rarely debate taking responsibility for the 'care' of others.

'The person who is most cared for, is the person who cares for themselves.'

If we care for ourselves and get it right then we become less of a burden for others. Our sense of our own value can be enhanced by being kind to ourselves first and foremost. It is not selfish. It is highly pragmatic since, if you are well, calm and confident, you are better able to help others for the right reason – not because you need to prove anything. And it also means that others have to spend less time taking 'care' of you. You are doing them a favour!

'By being kind to yourself you are being kind to others.'
Julia Cameron

Remember too that you are unique. There has only ever been and will only ever be one 'you'. Give that unique individual your time. Give yourself the time to consider who and what you are, what you wish for, what concerns you and what influences you. You cannot take this project seriously until you take yourself seriously. It is by no means selfish to be self-aware.

'Men go abroad to wonder at the height of mountains, at the huge waves of the sea, at the long courses of the rivers, at the vast compasses of the ocean, at the circular motion of the stars, and they pass by themselves without wondering.'
Augustine of Hippo

WAY 3 Preparing for change

For any of this to work, you must be able to cope with change. More than that, you will need to 'direct' the change. Change is inevitable in life. Ageing, starting from the moment we are born, is a fundamental part of being human. Ageing produces constant change in the body but that is supported by a physiological system of 'homeostasis' which strives to maintain some stability in the functions of our body as it changes through life and as it tries to stay in balance with our immediate environment. Homeostasis is a natural attempt at maintaining balance or equilibrium in our body. In the same way you can strive to maintain balance and that core stability as you meet the inevitable changes in life.

Our resistance to change is often linked to a previous sense of failure. Look back at chances you have taken in the past. When they were successful why were they? When they failed, what were the causes of failure? Examine these in detail – inspect your feelings about them too.

List the things you think you failed at.

List the reasons why you think you failed.

List the things you accomplished successfully.

List the reasons you were successful.

If things went wrong did you immediately make changes, or did you stick at them? Why? Examine what you risk by taking the chance to allow and adapt to change. What emotional, financial, or material losses do you risk?

All too often it is in relationships with other people that we find difficulties in allowing change. For example, have you lost out by telling people what your feelings are? Do people not respond as you hope or expect them to do so? Do people not respect the plans you have for your life and future?

Sometimes, when you have a new idea or plan about your direction in life and you tell old friends they say: 'But you always used to...'

When I became vegetarian and told friends about it they would say: 'But you love the taste of meat!' Well I did. But it wasn't a loss of taste that led to my new dietary conviction – it was a moral choice about not killing animals unnecessarily. So, yes, I did enjoy the taste of meat, but I can't enjoy it any longer when I know it requires the unnecessary death of an animal.

In any case my friends and associates should equally allow for the fact that tastes can change. I no longer enjoy the sugary delights that I indulged in as a child. I no longer appreciate the television or radio programmes that once gave me great pleasure. Have you ever tried re-reading a book you read some years earlier? Some books that gave me pleasure no longer stir my interest when I try to read them again. Yet other books I once tried and 'couldn't get in to' mean much more to me when I try again at a later date. So notice when someone says: 'But you used to...' And, more importantly, resist applying that limitation to yourself.

> **TIP:** Remember these lines for coping with change...
>
> **Every day is different.**
>
> **Today is an entirely new day.**
>
> **You don't have to want or need today what you desired yesterday.**

Remember not to seek gratification for your plans or your achievements from others. They rarely fully appreciate or acknowledge your success. All too often people resent others' success. They sometimes think successful people should be 'taken down a peg or two'. At other times we hold on to a belief that some pernicious force is deliberately setting up obstacles to our doing well in life. There must be a little imp or pixie whose sole function is to make things difficult for us – your shoelaces keep coming undone (it's the shoelace pixie!); your hat keeps getting blown off (it's the hat gnome!); you keep dropping your glove (it's the glove imp!).

Other people who do give you problems may not be able to help themselves. There is little use in being angry with them. They have to deal with their own problems. You must address your own.

You may be concerned about the idea of change. You may even feel challenged by the very word 'change' itself. If so remember that our lives are inevitably in a state of flux – instead think in terms of your 'growth' and 'development'. Stability and harmony can come from recognising the enjoyment of not only 'going with the flow' but steering the flow for yourself.

'A new life begins for us with every second. Let us go forward joyously to meet it. We must press on, whether we will or not, and we shall walk better with our eyes before us than with them ever cast behind.'
Jerome K. Jerome

WAY 4 Presenting your self

I don't want you to pretend to be something you are not ... but sometimes pretending to be something or someone that *you aspire to* can help you get there.

TIP: 'Present' your 'self' to others...

...put your 'self' in the present and 'make a present' of your self.

Therapist Virginia Satir (1976) explained how words are important 'contact' tools. When we produce words 'All the senses, the nervous system, brain, vocal cords, throat, lungs and all parts of the mouth are involved... physiologically talking is a very complicated process.' The problem is we do this so automatically that we often don't take enough care over the production process. For example, she asks: 'Do you know how your face looks right now?

Do you know how your voice sounds at this moment? You probably don't, but everyone looking at you and hearing you does.' They are taking their cues from 'reading' your external presentation – they are taking cues from what you say and how you look. They read your outside while you are aware of your inside. But sometimes these don't match and that's why misunderstanding occurs.

If someone says you seem unhappy or angry and you don't think you are, go immediately and look in a mirror. Check out the evidence behind their judgement. We often do not realise how we 'come across' to others. You might be surprised that you do 'seem' angry or unhappy even if that is not what you intend or how you feel.

Speaking in public is a performance. I once worked in an organisation where most visitors seemed a little dissatisfied, even unhappy, when they came to meet me. I had a friend walk through the reception area and they told me the main problem was that the receptionist did not greet them well. She did not look at them or smile or say anything much. The receptionist was a novice but someone should have explained to her that the greeting a visitor receives colours their whole first impression of the organisation. A receptionist is a more vital element of corporate image than most people recognise. I found a way to advise the novice receptionist and suggested she started to look people in the eye, smile and simply say: 'Can I help you?' It looked a little artificial at first but she soon overcame her shyness as people responded in like fashion. In a short time she became extremely adept at this greeting ritual and the attitudes of visitors changed completely.

So, whatever your position in an organisation, or even just socially or when in a shop buying something, always introduce yourself with a smile. If it's appropriate say your name and greet people with a gentle but firm handshake. Now that I live in France I see a remarkable cultural difference in greeting rituals. When you walk into a shop in my local town you are greeted by the staff, and often by the customers with a: 'Bonjour...monsieur, madame.' These are not people I know! The postman shakes hands with me every day I meet him. And people of acquaintance greet with a kiss on both cheeks. Indeed kissing an acquaintance on the cheek has increased in the UK too. Such gestures are ways of oiling the social machine, of smoothing out the fabric of our lives. It is a way of establishing the harmony of a relationship before we get down to the business of what we are there to do or buy.

Words are even more powerful and we need to watch how we use them and how others are using them. Think about how you use pronouns. We tend to avoid using the word 'I' since it might seem to sound self-centred. But we should not avoid it when we honestly need to put across our own view: 'I think...' Even the use of the word 'you' can sound critical such as in: 'You are making things worse.' However if you say: 'I think you are making things worse', it softens the sense of accusation.

The worst 'word culprits' are 'always' and 'never'. They are rarely used in a literal sense,

rather express an extreme emotion such as in: 'You always make me mad.' Or 'You never do as I ask.' Take particular note of: 'You always used to...' It is rarely the case that people either 'always' or 'never' do something.

Others might slip into using these phrases, so make sure that you don't use them. Examine how you use words and avoid using them casually if you can. Think more about how you communicate with others. Begin by talking slowly and remember to breathe. A few simple deep breaths in private can help to prepare you for a stressful meeting. Warm up your voice before you need to use it publicly. Some people find singing or chanting helps. (I advise doing that in private!)

Before you speak capture people's attention. Give them time to look at you before they listen. If you wish to maintain their attention, speak clearly and concisely. And remember to listen equally carefully to what they have to say. Let them know you are interested in them.

You will have come across the words 'extrovert' and 'introvert'. I want to make it clear that I don't think you should try to change the fundamental 'you' – we are looking for the modifications that will help you lead a contented life. Whichever you are, it is part of your core self. If you are something of an introvert I am not trying to suggest that you should 'get out more'. We all need to recognise these parts of our personality and make the adjustments necessary for a contented life. Laurie Helgoe (2013) has written an important book to help introverts manage their life in what she sees is our fundamentally extrovert world. It is almost as if 'introversion' is treated as a mental illness in a society which requires us to be more outgoing. She advises that introverts need quiet time for reflection and contemplation before they interact with others. Extroverts rush headlong into things and seek the company of others; introverts avoid too much social interaction. So if you see yourself as an introvert do not force yourself to meet the demands of an extrovert-dominated world. Allow yourself the time to retreat and gather your thoughts before engaging with others – and you will then be able to do so in a balanced and measured way. (Indeed extroverts could gain a lot from similarly taking time for thought and contemplation.)

Presenting yourself is a form of communication and, when you do it, you certainly will want it to be 'effective'.

Think about the three 'A's:

- Who is your **A**udience?
- What is your **A**im?
- What do you hope to **A**chieve?

Quite simply this means thinking about 'who' you are communicating with, what you are trying to 'say' to them and what you hope the 'outcome' will be.

Take the example of 'presenting your self' to a person you have not met before. Your 'audience' will not know much about you. In which case your aim might be to let them know something about you that is relevant to this new relationship – such as the possibility that there may be some mutual benefit in you knowing each other. In which case what you hope to achieve will be the thought in the mind of the other person that you are 'worth' knowing.

'Connecting' with your audience – whether that is one person, a group or 100 people in a lecture theatre – requires a range of skills. Some skills come naturally, others improve with practice.

At first just watch and listen. Be interested in them and attend to what they say and what they do. In some situations you may not even be required to speak, but how you listen to others will be seen as a concern for them, for who *they* are. On occasion all you may have to do is 'be present'. Simply be there and with them. Be sensitive to the social 'atmosphere' and try to spot any of the social rules or customs in operation.

The next step up is to connect with your audience. Ironically this means that the effective 'presentation of your self' requires that, for the time being, you forget about your 'self' and think of their 'selves'. To show interest ask them questions and take notice of their responses.

People who have problems in 'public speaking' – or even just in talking to other people – often do so because they are thinking about their own self too much: What if I make a mistake? Or – Will I make a fool of myself? Or be embarrassed?

Forget your 'self':

...listen ...observe ...be warm ...ask questions and
...be ready to talk about your self if necessary.

In this way your own self will emerge naturally and with ease.

1 2 3 4 **5 6** 7 8
9 10 11 12 13 14
15 16 17 18 19
20 21 22 23 24
25 26 27 28 29
30 31 32 33 34
35 36 37 38 39
40 41 42 43 44
45 46 47 48 49

Chapter 2

© depositphotos.com

'You are not in this world to live up to other people's expectations,
nor should you feel the world must live up to yours.'

Fritz Perl

WAY 5 Voices of doom

I particularly enjoyed a Woody Allen film called *Mighty Aphrodite* in which, every now and then, a Greek Chorus would appear with messages of foreboding and doom. Dressed in the contemporary costume of Ancient Greece and speaking in an archaic language style, they conveyed authentically the kinds of doubts and thoughts that had occurred to the character in the movie. Of course they were not supposed to be seen as 'real'. Rather they represented the thoughts, doubts and concerns of those characters. It was a reminder that other people cannot make you unhappy. But what you tell yourself can do that. The internal dialogue (which constitutes thinking) is between your self and a Greek Chorus, or constantly 'chattering voices' that are difficult to silence. Such voices may dominate to such an extent that they impede intuitive action by interfering with your 'flow' of creativity (Csikszentmihalyi, 1996), or they become your doubting 'inner game' (Gallwey, 1975). Or they are simply constantly negative, acting as what Julia Cameron sees as an internal censor. These are the 'Who do you think you are?' doubts that haunt most of us from time to time.

Personal developers give a great deal of instruction about what you should and should not say to yourself. You either have to listen to what the chattering voices say and find a way to answer back or learn to completely ignore them. You must continually accentuate the positive. The positive nature of self-development language stands in sharp contrast to the negative messages and content of ordinary everyday speech or conversation, this, of course, being the true source of the Greek Chorus. People like to complain. So negative narratives cultivate negative emotions that set up a downward spiral for mind and body. Positive accounts and consequent emotions boost physical and mental health. The problem is how to avoid the negative statements which can be so deeply embedded in our culture. Never allow the chattering voices to dominate your thoughts or the Greek Chorus to warn you so much that you are led to inactivity. You must always talk to yourself in a positive way.

Coué would have us repeat: 'Every day, **in every respect**, I am getting better and better' to ourselves twenty times every morning (Coué 1960: 23).

Louise Hay offers a range of healing affirmations to be repeated in this way, such as: 'Everything I touch is a success.' (Hay 1984: 150–88).

Try this

To lessen our pain and to gain power Susan Jeffers says we have to change our language and choose our vocabulary carefully (1987: 39): we never say 'should', instead we 'could' do something if we wished. We don't say 'can't', but we might say 'won't'. Our 'problems' have to be seen as 'opportunities'; 'if only' becomes 'next time'. By monitoring our words, and eliminating the negatives, we steadily expand the area of respite and silence from the chattering voices.

Now this can actually be very difficult to do in a sustained way. It can be almost 'Pollyanna-ish'. Thus when I have a problem with my car, I have real difficulty turning that 'challenge' into an opportunity. The next time my car develops an 'opportunity', by having a broken windscreen or a flat tyre, I know I'll struggle to remind myself that I 'can' take the opportunity to remember how to change a wheel or be educated in modern methods of windscreen replacement.

There is a joke about two students about to enter an exam:

A says: 'I think I'm going to fail.'

A's friend (who has read self-help literature) says: 'You must be more positive.'

A says: 'OK... I AM going to fail.'

Remember that persistence can reap tremendous benefits. Robert Pirsig collected a series of placid reflections on his broken down old motorbike and his relationship with his son, linked them to his thoughts about philosophy and produced both a philosophical treatise on the nature of the scientific method and a cult book that sold in the millions – *Zen and the Art of Motorcycle Maintenance*. Or when Richard Bach wrote *Jonathan Livingston Seagull*, inspired by his life as a stunt pilot, he was travelling around making very little money and his agent struggled to find him to tell him he'd written a bestseller. The book made him a fortune.

> 'Diamonds are only lumps of coal that stuck to their jobs.'
> *B.C. Forbes*

The voices of doom for many people are found in the workplace. There was an old notice you often saw in offices and factories: YOU DON'T HAVE TO BE CRAZY TO WORK HERE – BUT IT HELPS. The truth behind that notice is that we often seem to find some things that we do at work to be 'crazy' – inappropriate rules, excessive forms to fill in and mindless bureaucracy. But the 'system' is so big that we find it difficult to do much about it. If you work in a large organisation it is tempting to imagine an oppressive hierarchy that needs to keep you in your place. The Greek Chorus will then come along and chant: 'Know your place. Don't upset the apple cart. Keep your head down. Do as you are told. Toe the line.' And so on. What you have to remember is that the 'system' is composed of other people. And the 'system' might not be just a work organisation; it can be your family, a community or the whole society. Communities can be just as oppressive and have just as much need to keep you 'in your place' as work organisations.

In fact there is no such thing as a 'community' – no 'thing' that is. It is perhaps the only view I held in common with the former British Prime Minister Margaret Thatcher when she said there was no such thing as society. Communities and societies exist as an idea in our heads. We experience them as 'real things' only through the people that go to make them up. So take note of the voices of doom that are essentially produced by other people and that suggest you should take care not to step out of line. The dangers they fear are coming from their own voices of doom. Their negativity arises out of the fact that they do not feel they can do anything about their situation. You do not need to adopt that negativity. Your new positive self can rise above it and see it for what it is.

Given the stress and pace of the modern work environment, people find themselves insecure and fearful of their colleagues' intentions. Counter this by assuming the best of people. Most people are only doing the best they can in the circumstances. When I deal with government bureaucracy, I do not deal with the 'thing' because it only exists as an idea in my head. I deal with a *person* behind a counter or on the telephone who 'represents' that organisation. Start by assuming they are doing their best. You may come across people who are deliberately doing their worst or who even have some malicious intent. But that tends not to happen too often. It is better to have occasional disappointment than constant suspicion. We can never fully know other people's real motives or the things that bother them. But we only harm ourselves if we are constantly suspicious of others. We can only begin to know our own motives.

'When another person makes you suffer, it is because he suffers deeply within himself, and his suffering is spilling over. He does not need punishment; he needs help. That's the message he is sending.'
Thich Nhat Hanh

WAY 6 Whose voice?

Look out for whose voice it is that you 'hear' in your head. Most people have their parents' or guardians' voices running a track in their mind – advising, guiding, warning or perhaps admonishing. If these are gentle, loving voices you are fortunate and they can be very supportive. Other voices can be negative. They might be 'put downs' which are hard to challenge. By the end of this project the voice you hear will be your own. It might have elements from earlier loving, caring other voices – you can choose – but you will be able to challenge any remaining negative voices since you will have acquired resources of your own. In some respects most of this book is about changing that voice. It is about developing your own voice, and building one that supports, guides, comforts and never criticises or admonishes.

I don't intend to focus much on families in this book. Everything we cover together can be applied to relationships within the family – to family 'life'. But as Virginia Satir explained, families 'make' people, so it is vital to understand how they go about this 'peoplemaking'. She showed how the family is the source of our self-worth. It teaches us fundamental forms of communication; which is how we construct meaning in the world. It gives us our first set of rules for how to behave and it establishes our relationships with the rest of society.

As a result some of the more dominant voices that we hear from our Greek Chorus are likely to be those of family members. If we are lucky those voices enhance our sense of worthiness, encourage us to communicate clearly and directly and honestly, lay down constructive and supportive rules to guide our lives and link us to the outside world in a mutually supportive and fulfilling way. If we are unlucky in the family 'factory' we find ourselves in, then the opposites hold: we are undervalued and feel worthless, communications are vague and largely critical, the rules are misguided and our relationships with the outside world flawed. It is precisely those negative voices that this book seeks to challenge.

Satir was not the only therapist to write about the influence of families in our lives. The psychiatrist R.D. Laing showed how the faulty communications processes found in some families could create schizophrenia in vulnerable family members. His colleague David Cooper believed that families would eventually disappear as a form of social organisation. Together these therapists offered a range of ways to address any negative influences coming from our families. All essentially advised learning to ignore the negative family voice, and instead to cultivate your own voice. None of this means necessarily having to leave your family behind, nor does it mean having to forget about them. More importantly, it is about understanding how they came to 'make' you what you are. Instead of rejecting them it helps to remain aware of their influence and see the voices they have produced for you.

> **TIP:** Think about the many other sources of the voices in our head:
>
> You ARE what you read.
>
> You ARE what you listen to.
>
> You ARE what you watch.

Those people I come across who read only the less serious newspapers, for example, hold 'tabloid views'. They often offer simple short arguments of prejudice that draw on the newspaper's editorial policy. There is little substance to their views and weak evidence to support them. But, perhaps for that reason, they hold on to them most tenaciously.

I had a good friend who had separated from her husband but was having difficulty in 'moving on'. Instead she was becoming increasingly depressed. While having a lift in her car I noticed that the only music she had was country music. Now there are not a lot of happy tunes in country music. It is usually about lost or unrequited love, about betrayal and death. I suggested she start listening to something more uplifting and preferably without words. So she abandoned the country for the classical and the change was almost immediate.

'Extraordinary how potent cheap music is.'
Amanda in Private Lives *(1930) by Noel Coward*

An even stronger subliminal influence upon our thoughts and behaviour is television. Neil Postman was a fierce critic of the power of television. In *The Disappearance of Childhood* (1982) he argued that television erodes the boundaries between children and adults, making children apathetic, cynical 'pseudo-adults' at the same time as infantilising adults. Later he expounded Aldous Huxley's fears of a 'Brave New World' in which '...people come to love their oppression, to adore the technologies that undo their capacities to think.' (1986: vii) And television, primarily as entertainment, has the power to do just that. There is a reason why it is so easy to become a 'couch potato' under the seduction of the television. The producers of television programmes do not want you to think, turn off the TV and take action. They want, indeed they *need* you to keep watching. It drugs you into complacency and into repeating the catchy phrases in advertisements and from TV 'personalities' in casual conversation. Instead of thinking of a response of our own, it becomes too easy to fall back on a TV cliché.

Jerry Mander (1992) writes of television as a 'technology that induces passivity'. Because people spend so much time watching it, it has effectively replaced the more active community participations of previous generations. It limits our potential for more diverse cultural pursuits and even a more active engagement with family life. The American TV production system is so slick and advanced that it has generated a cultural imperialism, a global domination that is in danger of producing a monoculture with little room for the rich and meaningful variety of cultural experiences that were previously spread around the world. Mander particularly bemoans the loss of 'native' cultural traditions across the globe as a consequence of the power of television.

Needing to access the news on the radio or TV every day can become an obsession. You may feel deprived without it. But 'no news is good news'. News thrives on conflict and adversity. You can reduce the tensions and stresses in your life if you go on retreat from the radio or TV for a while. You'll be surprised how little has changed if you leave it for a few days. All news forms have to make you believe that you will be missing something if you don't keep up. Unless you are a politician or a diplomat you probably won't be missing much and, in any case, catching up is easy since news stories are recorded, repeated and sustained as long as there is media interest.

'Sometimes when I can't go to sleep at night I see the family of the future. Dressed in three-tone shorts-and-shirt sets of disposable Papersilk, they sit before the television wall of their apartment, only their eyes moving. After I've looked a while I always see – otherwise I'd die – a pigheaded soul over in the corner with a book; only his eyes are moving, but in them there is a different look.'
Randall Jarrell

Of course these days there are many more screen-based technologies that 'undo our capacities to think'. We have laptops, smartphones, tablets and all sorts of gaming devices that lock us into interacting with them. Add the power and lure of the Internet accessed

from these devices that enables us to play games, access up-to-date news from around the world, and get information about anything, whatever the time and wherever we happen to be. To say nothing of virtual reality games with surround sound headsets and the advent of 3D retinal projection headsets where images are projected directly onto the retina. All these devices demand our undivided attention, and often receive it. But remember that communications technology, like all technologies, is neutral. Whether or not it has a positive or negative impact depends upon how we use it or adapt it. A spade can be a digging tool, or a weapon in the 'wrong' hands. Similarly, communications technologies can be of great benefit if we think carefully about how we use them.

For ten years my wife and I didn't have a television. And it was one of our most productive periods. We wrote and we read much more than ever before. The capture of your concentration tends not to happen with books since you are in control in reading a book. If you are not enjoying it you can more easily stop, put it down and try another book.

If you are fully engaged you tend to read it quickly and the dialogue you have with it is in your own head. I find that some books provoke so much thinking that I read them more slowly, since I have to stop and think and develop my own views. At other times I read a book 'selectively', dipping in where I see a heading that looks interesting or a topic that is relevant.

'A book is the only place in which you can examine a fragile thought without breaking it, or explore an explosive idea without fear it will go off in your face... It is one of the few havens remaining where [your] mind can get both provocation and privacy.'
Edward P. Morgan

I am not suggesting that you should never watch television or listen to the radio or play popular music. Nor am I suggesting that you ignore the wizardry offered by modern communications technologies. I am suggesting that you should access all these media selectively – as you might with a book.

> **Try this**
>
> Make a daily plan for your watching, listening, gaming, web-surfing and so on in ways that allow time for other thoughtful pursuits as well. Decide in advance how much time you will spend watching TV and when. Timetable your Internet access or your social media interacting. Such a plan helps avoid merely 'drifting' into mindless interactions or the passive receipt of someone else's messages.

If you do not run your subconscious mind yourself, someone else will run it for you. Regain control of these voices. You can control them; don't let them control you.

'It is only by the love of reading that the evil resulting from the association with little minds can be counteracted.'
Elizabeth Hamilton

'Books are the quietest and most constant of friends; they are the most accessible and wisest of counsellors, and the most patient of teachers.'
Charles W. Eliot

TIP: With all communications media – even books – put them down from time to time, look into the distance and contemplate the trees, the sky, buildings and people passing by. Let your thoughts drift wherever they will and make space in your mind away from the constant stream of other people's messages.

1 2 3 4 5 6 **7 8**
9 10 11 12 13 14
15 16 17 18 19
20 21 22 23 24
25 26 27 28 29
30 31 32 33 34
35 36 37 38 39
40 41 42 43 44
45 46 47 48 49

Chapter 3

STEPS TO SUCCESS: HAVING A PLAN

'Sapiens quidem pol ipse fingit fortunam sibi.'

(The wise carve their own fate.)

Plautus

WAY 7 Mission statement

Throughout this book I will suggest writing things down. Writing can be a vital step in clarifying your thoughts and your intentions. The worst place in the world to store an idea is in the head. It has to compete with too many other ideas there and so might get lost. Instead write down what you want to achieve and how you plan to do it.

You can place your writing in several different locations. Some people keep a diary or journal which they write in daily. It can be a way of organising your ideas about things or reflecting upon the events in your life – in your own time without subjecting yourself to the pressures put on by other people. For the exercises in this book you might try keeping one attractive, hardback notebook in which you write down your responses to my suggestions. I say 'write' since there are times when putting a pen to paper and seeing the actions of your hand and the emergence of the words on the page cannot be substituted by typing into a computer. Jackee Holder discusses this in her book *49 Ways to Write Yourself Well* (2013). Choose the colour and size of your book carefully; make it something you wish to pick up and use. Make the ink a favourite colour. I like black; my wife prefers sepia.

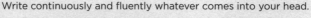

Try this

Every day, at a regular time which is convenient for you, write either a specified amount of words (say a page) or for a specific length of time. Write continuously and fluently whatever comes into your head. Don't pause to correct grammar or style, just let it flow. There is no need to go back over it and read it. The exercise of writing clears the head and focuses your thoughts. You might also be surprised at your insights if you keep the writings and go back to them months, or even years, later. But it can be equally as helpful to throw them away at regular intervals, for example when the book is full. You choose.

In a world in which most of us are obliged to use computers on a daily basis it can be a valuable sensory delight to use the old-fashioned pen-to-paper method. But it is the writing that is important so if you prefer to write into your computer then do so. What matters is that writing can be a first step in 'taking aim'. Success in whatever you seek cannot be achieved if you are 'aim-less'.

In my clinical therapy work the first thing I would ask a client is: 'Exactly what is it you want to achieve?' I found this to be the crucial question. It was essential to guiding the therapy. What was surprising to me then was how often people did not actually know what they wanted to achieve. They sensed a dissatisfaction, discontentment or concern. But they did not have a precise 'goal' as such.

If you don't know where you want to be, how will you know when you get there? It is important to formulate your goals.

Before you begin to refine your goals, it helps to design the means and methods you feel appropriate to moving you to that goal. So have a personal 'mission statement', or a motto that is uniquely yours. Write it down and look at it daily.

When in my middle teens I decided upon a motto. I wrote it neatly on a card and placed it on a bookshelf in full sight. I saw it every day. It offered guiding principles for me.

> **TIP:** Write your own motto and keep it displayed for you to catch sight of from time to time. Mine was like this:
>
> **Be honest.**
> **Be independent.**
> **Be authentic.**
> **Be kind.**

Now, I realise that I cannot be entirely independent. We are all in some form of interdependence since we are social beings. And I have to admit that I haven't always been as honest or as kind as I would like. But this motto was my 'steer' and when I did make mistakes I knew what I had to come back to in order to adjust my aim. For people who need to go on the journey, the mission statement is a kind of map. If you can see life as a journey, then you need a map and you need to decide upon your destination. To go towards your destiny you need a map to define the territory and to work out a route. Side trips off the route are allowed so long as they do not distract you from reaching your destination, and so long as they make some contribution to you reaching your goal. As with any journey there may be costs to taking the side trips.

You may have to decide to take an express route or the tourist route. If you are 20 years old, and don't mind some diversions on the way to a goal you might attain when you are 50, then take the tourist route. If you are 50 and have been diverted too many times in the past then plan an express route to your destination. Even in our later years we still need to map the future. What matters is your choice of how you travel and what your destination is for. Personally I like time to consider and take in the sights. Once I travelled in Italy with a friend who is an avid traveller. Normally I would see, say, one cathedral and a town centre in a day. It would take me that long to digest those places. With him I visited three churches and two different towns – in one day. I was exhausted, physically and mentally, and I retained little useful information from what I had seen. I was in a whirl. He was delighted by the number of places he had been to.

So think about how *you* wish to travel and then start to set out your goals and write them down. Recently I found a note of my own goals that was written on 9 April 1999. I wrote: *I will make a very good living as a writer, lecturer and clinical hypnotherapist*. I had a clinical practice for 12 years, I continued to lecture and write subsequently. These days I lecture less and I write a great deal more. But those goals have been achieved.

Conduct your own personal 'vision workshop'.

Write down what you are doing now.
What is good about it?
What is not so good about it?

Write down where you desire to be and
what you desire to be doing...

...next week
...next year
...in ten years' time.

Which of the things you are doing now will help you move towards the things you desire?

Keep doing them.

Which will not help?

As soon as you are able, stop doing them.

Now start to think about what extra things you need to achieve those goals.

One device often suggested for formulating goals and the means for getting there is to write your own epitaph. It is a way of working back from the future.

Think about what you would be content to have accomplished at the end of your life.

I would be happy with the following epitaph:

RON WAS A KIND AND HONOURABLE PERSON WHO WAS A DELIGHT TO KNOW. HE WAS A GOOD AND CONSIDERATE FRIEND.

Now write your own epitaph.

Try this

....

WAS

....

....

....

....

....

The actual future we will live is a combination of our desired future and the range of all possible futures. Desires and possibilities are the means through which we will achieve the future. In fact it is best not to talk about 'the' future, since it implies that there is only one future and it is already set. There are, right now, many possible futures for each of us. We could choose simply to let things happen and see which future turns up. Which means that we would be letting the future be almost randomly chosen from the set of possible futures and it is, therefore, very unlikely to come close to our desired future. Why should it?

In many cases this might even mean that we end up living the lives that others have expected of us or chosen for us. It is 'vital' – and that means 'life-giving' – to think about and to plan for the future. We need to consider the range of possible outcomes, choose which ones we prefer and actively seek to achieve those outcomes. Thinking and planning does require some effort, but not an extraordinary amount. It involves simply enough effort to break the bad habit of complacency. It is the kind of effort that stops us from becoming mere victims of a random future.

WAY 8
Keep a list

Pulling yourself together is not a chore, even though the practical suggestions made here may at times seem a little mundane. In fact, together we are seeking to bring enchantment back into your life. Writer and lecturer Thomas Moore has shown how attention to the mundane detail of everyday life is ironically part of its re-enchantment. By looking at what you do now and making it magical, your attitudes to the mundane will be transformed. By adopting these simple devices of a formulaic nature the details of your life become more valued and, as a consequence, life will 'magically' change. These include the reflections upon your self that I suggested earlier and contemplation of the consequences of your actions, or the regular writing of 'daily pages' in your journal (Reynolds 1991: 24–8, Cameron 1994: 9).

Lists are of great practical use. Write your lists down in a form you know you can easily look at. I still use coloured 'Post-Its'. What a brilliant invention that was! Even the reminders you find as 'apps' on phones, tablets and computers are often in the form of sticky notes in a range of colours. Number the tasks to be done in priority order. Once the tasks you have to complete are on a list you don't have to keep remembering them. You can 'clear your head'.

TIP: These are the essential things to remember about lists...

1) Write each item or task clearly.
2) Have a 'manageable' number of tasks on each list – never too many.
3) Remember to look at them from time to time to remind yourself of the tasks to be accomplished.
4) Remember to take them with you when you are on your way to do any of the tasks.

You can have lists for the major goals in your life as well as when you are going shopping for groceries. Again this seems such a simple, mundane thing to do, and something we often will do for shopping, but forget to do for other more important aspects of our life. You should have started to think about how you wish to travel through life. So now it is time to define your destination. Write down a list of your goals. You will need to be specific, and positively realistic. You might already know what these are, but if you are not sure how to go about doing this:

Every now and then, close your eyes and imagine yourself as having achieved some or all of your main goals. See yourself in your mind's eye as having achieved just what you set out to achieve.

Imagine where you are physically. Examine the location, the room, the climate and so on. Think about what you are doing and what you have done.

Try this

The bigger goals are only achieved in several smaller steps. Each of these little steps is important and requires the same attention as the bigger goals. So you can even imagine how you would feel, what you would think, what you might say to people after accomplishing some smaller tasks such as, say, passing a test, succeeding at a job interview, or doing a particular job well.

I do this even with a small project in the garden. I have in mind a particular garden overall. It must be easy to manage, pleasant to look at and a pleasure to be in and use. As part of that overall project I need to build some dry stone walls to contain certain shrubs. So I imagine the wall as having been built, the shrubs planted and me looking at the finished garden with this wall in it. That way I can focus on building the wall successfully since I know clearly what I am aiming at.

I keep my 'garden project' goal in a neat black notebook and my smaller task lists in there too. But every day you will need to remind yourself of your goals and the little steps needed to move towards the main goal. So look at your lists of goals in the morning before the demanding duties of the day take over. Look at your written goals. Add to them if you want or even re-write them in order to refresh your

interest in and commitment to them. But don't rush this process. Be patient and let them steadily emerge over time.

It may help to share your goals with someone you trust to act as a mentor. But if you do this you must choose this individual very carefully. It must be someone you know will be supportive of your goals and is keen to help you review them regularly. 'Reporting' your achievements to them can be a great motivator and when things are going more slowly they may even help in reviving your commitment or putting you in touch with others who can help.

Most of the problems we have in life are related to how we learn things. In some ways what we are doing here is learning how to:

- alter our attitudes
- improve our thoughts

which all helps to...

- modify our behaviour.

The first 20 years of my professional life were spent dealing with adult learners – often with people who felt they were 'square pegs in round holes'. When they tried to learn things anew their unfamiliarity with learning led them to feel at times that they were 'knitting fog', as one of my students used to say. I soon discovered that I had to offer them simple devices for organising their thoughts: how to take notes, how to file them, how to structure an essay and how to plan for passing exams.

This is why I suggest the simple devices above for enhancing the manageability of this self-development project. By linking to the mundane aspects of daily life, envisioned distant outcomes are made achievable. By encouraging a focus upon everyday life, and by framing it as a natural part of your daily activities, you will be taking the critical first steps. These simple exercises are crucial to taking action.

© freepik.com

WAY 9

Plan the day, week and year

Planning your day, your week, your month, your year and so on is essential. By now you will be on your way to clarifying what you are really aiming at – your valued goals. You will have written down your goals to help maintain your focus and to avoid being sidetracked. While you need to be very precise and very specific about your goals, you also need to be realistic so that they are achievable by your own efforts and not dependent on the actions of others. Put your focus on those things that you can control. If you focus on the realistically unattainable you become dependent upon what others may permit.

Set yourself a timetable and think of being realistic. Remember to begin by setting out the smaller steps that you have to go through to achieve those larger goals. Also write these down, even the small things, in the order in which they will have to be done to achieve the necessary results. Have a planned sequence of intermediate goals along the route to your chosen goals. These are the manageable small steps on the way to your ultimate destination. Goals must be measurable and observable. You must be able to demonstrate to yourself when you have achieved them, so this must be a proper schedule. As Dr. Phil McGraw says: 'Someday' is not a day of the week. A fixed calendar of events must be established. Be precise about when you are to do something and when a particular goal is completed.

It can help to think in terms of numbers. They hold a certain kind of magic. If there are not too many 'steps', 'stages' or 'levels' then you can have a sense of the manageability of the project. As a general rule the fewer steps the better. Find a number that matches the routines in your own life. The number seven is popular because it matches days of the week. If you like to have a daily routine throughout the week then establish seven habits, routines or steps towards your goals that you can repeat on a weekly cycle. Twelve (one a month) suggests a yearly calendar, while 365 neatly gives us an annual rotation of one a day for a year. *The Course in Miracles* offers 365 meditations to complete the course in one year (Foundation for Inner Peace, 1996). Thus I could plan to take 30 minutes each day to study and do a meditation and I know for certain that, at the end of the year, I will have completed the course.

In designing your own 'calendar' of events remember that there is no rush. It may take time to accomplish your cherished goals. So take that time. Enjoy the process of accomplishing, not only the accomplishment. That is what living your life is all about.

Decide on something you will plan to do every day. (For example, you will walk for at least ten minutes every day.)

Try this

Decide upon something you will do on a weekly basis. (So, Monday might be a day for shopping, Tuesday a day you go out with friends – and so on. It doesn't matter what you do as long as it fits into a schedule you commit to for yourself.)

Choose something you will permit yourself to do once a month. (You might go to the theatre or attend a concert or a show or go to the beach or a lake.)

The overarching lesson about success has to do with how to 'play the game'. Now is the time to decide, drawing upon all the ideas that I suggested above, what really matters to you. In this game of life do you want to win above all else, above all other considerations, or do you want to play the game well?

This decision is vital to how you proceed in the game of life. It can be quite easy simply to succeed at the expense of all other things. Work hard, day in day out, never see family or friends, make choices that have little to do with the interests of others, be ruthless, and you can succeed. You could make lots of money, be powerful and still have little time for others as you continue to win. On the other hand, if time with family and friends is important to you, if you enjoy their company, if that is what makes life worthwhile, then decide that now so that your priorities are clear.

For example, don't have children if you do not intend to enjoy them. They are demanding and have ongoing needs. Realise that now and commit. Don't seek friends if you view them as an obligation. Time with friends might only be an end in itself. It might only offer the pleasure of their company. But you are also likely to receive their opinions and their demands too! On the other hand friends and family can help

you accomplish your cherished goals. Don't assume they won't; simply decide and act on the basis of that decision.

Let's take my writing of this book as an example. Alongside all the other things in my life, I wanted to finish writing this book. It is quite an important goal to me and fits into my overall aspiration to write and connect with people. The deadline is two months away. I calculated that, if I write for three hours every day, the book will be finished in good time. I write better in the mornings so those three hours are best taken up in the morning. Now, a good friend wanted to take me into the nearest town, spend the day there, have lunch and so on – and I haven't seen her for a while. However, that would mean I would need to find another three hours on another day which would interfere with other plans, and if I write for six hours on one day I know I won't write so well as if I only write for three hours a day and use the rest of the day for other leisure and thinking and reading. I explained that to my friend and since she is a good friend she understood and will wait until the book is finished. It is those friends who are not so 'good', who are less understanding, that I can do without. I have designed my timetable in the best possible way to achieve my desired goal. My 'good' friends will be patient and help me do that.

WAY 10 Prioritise

The management of time is the ultimate in self-control and the taking of personal responsibility. I have already suggested that you need to prioritise, but you may need help in deciding how to do this. Think in terms of two 'dimensions' of priority: urgency and importance. Your tasks will vary in terms of how urgent they are and how important they are. You can easily sketch a two by two table and place your tasks in the relevant quadrant and then number them within each box.

Very Urgent +

Quick and simple | Critical > Crisis

Not important | **Very important**

Time wasted | Planning

Not Urgent −

Once you have allocated tasks to each quadrant you can set about actually doing them. If you prioritise those things that are both not urgent and not important you will be literally 'wasting' time. It is often tempting to do the urgent but not important things if they can be done 'quickly and simply'. But there is little doubt that you will not be doing the tasks that are both very urgent and very important. Those things that are important but not very urgent can be placed in your long-term timetable so that you can plan when they can be done and when they need to be done by. If you do not attend to those things in the top right quadrant immediately you may be setting yourself up for a crisis. So, do those things first.

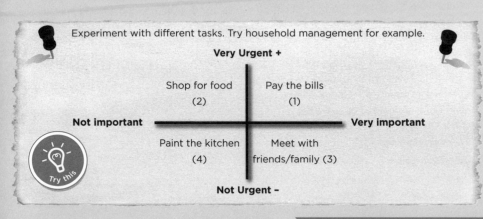

Experiment with different tasks. Try household management for example.

Very Urgent +

Shop for food (2) | Pay the bills (1)

Not important | **Very important**

Paint the kitchen (4) | Meet with friends/family (3)

Try this

Not Urgent −

Of course there will come a time when painting the kitchen becomes more important and takes on a certain urgency. So tasks do move around the quadrant if they have to be done at some time or other. The trick is to get them in the right order and do them. And don't forget that we sometimes get so involved with the 'urgent' tasks that we fail to do the most 'important' ones. So don't always prioritise urgency over importance.

'You have to live on this twenty-four hours of daily time. Out of it you have to spin health, pleasure, money, content, respect and the evolution of your immortal soul. Its right use, its most effective use, is a matter of the highest urgency and of the most thrilling actuality. All depends on that. We shall never have any more time.'
Arnold Bennett

Obviously how you fill in the time management quadrant depends upon your priorities. So try the following useful ideas for managing your time:

Write a list: of those areas in your life in which you feel insecure, which need attending to, which cause you fear and/or anxiety. With each one write down something you can do, immediately, to reduce the cause of your concern. Add those things to your list of priorities.

Prioritise: focus on the most important tasks – the things you really must get done today. Assign numbers to the tasks in the list. Number 1 must be the first thing you really must get done today!

Procrastination: What task(s) have you been putting off? Examine why and then give them a place in your list of priorities. When they crop up, do them according to their 'urgency' and 'importance'.

In meetings or appointments: To keep control, always go in with your own agenda. Decide beforehand what you want out of the meeting. Stay focused on achieving your goals. Recognise that others have their own goals. If they match yours that is great since you will be able to gain a consensus towards a collective goal. Sometimes people don't disclose their hidden agendas. And other people's agendas might not match yours. So sometimes it helps to declare your boundaries. Be clear about how long you can allow for the meeting. Keep meetings short. Often the key decisions only take place in the last 15 minutes of a meeting; so control the time accordingly. Ensure that meetings are time-bounded by subsequent 'urgent' and fixed appointments – such as lunch!

Only handle papers once: deal with their requirements when you pick them up, and file them when finished with or destroy them if you can.

Avoid timewasting ICT: The Internet and the World Wide Web are undoubtedly very useful but they can also be great timewasters, as I suggested earlier. Just like television it can be a seductive way to spend time. To control your time allocate times during the day when you will attend to e-mail; don't leave it on and watch it all the time. Replying immediately to text messages on your mobile can distract from more urgent tasks. You do not have to 'like' everyone on Facebook or thank everyone for recommending you on LinkedIn. Unsubscribe from non-essential newsgroups, lists or discussion forums. Think about letting the answerphone/voicemail take messages during the day while you attend to more urgent priorities.

'Your time is limited so don't waste it living someone else's life.'
Steve Jobs

Dealing with the casual visit: Find friendly, natural ways to end a conversation. People used to 'drop in' to my office 'for a chat' from time to time. Of course there are times when you need a break and can allow for that; but not if they are dictating your timetable and hindering your completion of vital tasks. I used to find a natural break in the conversation, rise from my chair and walk towards the door. Few people failed to get the implicit message that our casual chat was over. If necessary, accompany the visitor into the corridor. It's easier then to accomplish a conversational ending and polite parting.

Turning phones off and letting voicemail take a call is better than ignoring it. It's almost like having a servant who will let callers know you are not 'at home'. Obviously there will be times when you need to leave phones on during family crises, or if you need it to make you money or, indeed, to save you time. The point is to clearly decide your priorities and act accordingly.

'Time ought, above all other kinds of property, to be free from invasion, and yet there is no man who does not claim the power of wasting that time which is the right of others.'
Samuel Johnson

The best book on time management I have found is by Godefroy and Clark (1989). It contains lots of practical guidance and helps you prioritise tasks in order to better manage your time. Never leave time to its own devices. Time needs to be 'managed' for best effect. You can save time; you can spend time; but time need never be wasted.

WAY 11 Recognise a sunk fund

There are some life projects that you simply have to allow yourself to give up on. Those are 'sunk funds'. There are so many traditional aphorisms that challenge you not to give up, when in fact it may be the wisest thing to do: 'You've made your bed – now you have to lie in it!' *No* you don't! Get up out of it and make another bed somewhere else! Have the courage to abandon a long-cherished project that isn't working for you.

To decide to give up is not a failure; it can take courage and shows wisdom. Time and effort is not wasted if you have learned something from that project – even if you have only learned when to give up! You might have learned why the project could not have been successfully seen through. And that could help in not making similar errors in future. Obviously 'giving up' can look like failure since it challenges our self-esteem and our ability to admit a mistake.

I gave up on studying for a PhD in 1976. I needed to earn a living for my family. I was given a new supervisor and I didn't get on with him. Keeping up a full-time job and studying part-time left me no time to spend with my loved ones. So I didn't 'fail' in my PhD project, I simply decided to discontinue something that wasn't doing me any good at the time.

My wife used to say: 'Don't keep "flogging a dead horse" – because even if it does get up it will only stagger about!'

> **TIP:** Carefully examine your current 'projects' (plans, ideas, hopes, intentions) and decide, realistically, how likely it is they will come to fruition and whether or not your effort invested in them will be worth it. Be prepared to let drop those projects that, with mature reflection, are unlikely to 'pay dividends'.

If I had continued with the PhD I suspect it would not have been of the quality I wished. But I learned a great deal from not completing that first PhD. Nearly 25 years later I did complete another PhD, when the conditions were right for me. I chose my supervisor carefully, I allocated time with consideration for leisure and family, and I was earning enough to support my family while studying part-time.

There really is no such thing as failure. But fear of failure can be so great it can stop you achieving your joy. And that is only 'the fear': it hasn't even happened yet! If you fail at something then review how essential it was to your goals. Then consider that the failure was a way of suggesting that you might be on the wrong track and you might need to reconsider your aims.

'Success is not achieved by insuring against failure.'
Patrick Stewart

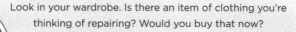

To give you some ideas about how to recognize a sunk fund:

Look in your wardrobe. Is there an item of clothing you're thinking of repairing? Would you buy that now?

Look at an item of your furniture you might be thinking of recovering. Would you buy it now?

You have a cherished car you have kept running for some years. It needs money spending on it to keep it on the road. Should you use your precious savings to keep it running, or use that money to invest in a newer car that you will be able to rely on?

The phrase 'throwing good money after bad' is apt. But it isn't just about wasting money – it may be expending time, energy or effort that is unlikely to be rewarded.

'Abandoned Sinclair C5' by Alan Gold from Polbeth, Scotland – Sinclair C5. Licensed under Creative Commons Attribution-Share Alike 2.0 via Wikimedia Commons – http://commons.wikimedia.org/wiki/File:Abandoned _Sinclair_C5.jpg#mediaviewer/File:Abandoned_ Sinclair_C5.jpg

1 2 3 4 5 6 7 8
9 10 11 **12 13** 14
15 16 17 18 19
20 21 22 23 24
25 26 27 28 29
30 31 32 33 34
35 36 37 38 39
40 41 42 43 44
45 46 47 48 49

Chapter 4

BELIEF BECOMES TRUTH

© depositphotos.com

'Whether you
believe you
can do a thing
or not, you
are right!'

Henry Ford

WAY 12 Thinking positive

'Positive words make us physically strong, negative words make us physically weak.'

Susan Jeffers

William James claimed that he learned from personal experience that how you act affects your emotions. He was countering a traditional view that if you are happy you will smile, with the idea that if you smile you will be happy. Indeed this is surprisingly easy to try from time to time.

Just smile: even if you are on your own. If you are feeling down or not 'getting on' with others in your life – just smile. The physical act of smiling induces endorphins; molecules in the brain that make us feel happy.

Coué's principles of autosuggestion were based on a particular view of the power of the mind over the will: 'Things are for us not what they are, but what they seem.' (Coué 1960: 34) Now we have increasing evidence that the mind does have direct physical effects on the body.

'Sometimes your joy is the source of your smile, but sometimes your smile can be the source of your joy.'

Thich Nhat Hanh

Not only does smiling trigger endorphins, simple aerobic activity also has this effect. The assumption here could that be the mere exercising of the facial muscles will bring about the desired response in improved health. (Tickling apparently does the same for some people.)

These traditional maxims have gained some scientific evidence with the recent popularity and successes of cognitive behavioural therapy (see Samways 1997). The direct links between the nervous and the immune systems are now well recognised. The study of what is known as psychoneuroimmunology has shown that both the brain and the immune system must be included in any attempt to account for the onset and course of human disease: 'Although the precise mechanisms whereby emotional distress can impair the immune system are not known, these interconnections provide a potential means by which psychological variables can influence health outcome'. (Hall, Altman and Blumenthal 1996: 11).

So this works both ways: some physical and emotional activities can help resist disease; others can actually create illness. The evidence for interconnectedness of mind and body, indeed the direct effects of mind on body, has been growing steadily (Martin 1997). There is now much more comprehensive awareness of the complex physiological basis for behavioural modification of the immune response at the body's cellular level. Some years ago Norman Cousins (1979) reported how he cured himself of a debilitating illness by watching comedy films. He reported how he laughed himself well, and we now understand the physiological mechanisms by which this worked.

In humans the most direct links to attitudes and beliefs, to emotions and behaviour, are narratives – the stories we tell ourselves, or others tell us, which are designed to encourage some form of improvement in our lives. Such stories are intended to influence our minds and bodies. They affect how we think, feel and act. Telling stories is a vital part of how we relate to the world and to each other. Characters, plots, endings and beginnings all convey notions about how the world is ordered.

In fact we are constructing a story in this book: the main character in the story is you. The plot embraces a conscious improvement or development of your self. By acting positively you will accomplish your main goals, while also attaining non-conscious outcomes such as general mental and physical health and well-being. As the main character in this story, your actions are vital – you must act now! By taking your part in this story you are also acting in harmony with what some see as the purpose of the cosmos, the universal good or what others regard as your divine destiny. Behaving in this way accepts the natural order of things and is rewarded.

One of the best ways to persuade you of this is in anecdotes of biographical success: the achievements of artists, poets, businessmen, and even politicians. Many of the personal development writers tell stories about the successful lives of others. In reading their accounts you can tell yourself: 'I can do that too!' And you learn more about what it entails from the personal disclosure of others; how they achieved their success. The maxims, metaphors and quotations of self-help and personal development are condensed narratives: apt and memorable aids to designing your progress by building upon the experiences of others.

Much of the literature has a lengthy tradition of stressing the powerful effects of belief upon the human mind and body. Regular affirmations in the form of positive accounts are encouraged (Waters 1996: 28). With exercises, effort and belief eyesight can be prevented from deterioration and even improved (Liberman 1995). Similarly exercises in self-regulation, visualisation and self-exhortation can extend your life and lead to direct health improvements via attitudinal change (Blakeslee 1997). For such reasons the importance of seeking the company of strong, motivated, inspirational people is often stressed (Jeffers 1987: 80).

As Coué counselled, if this is true then we must be mindful of what a physician is doing in telling a patient that they are suffering from an incurable illness and there is nothing more that can be done for them (Coué 1960: 24). What then is their potential for favourable outcomes? The body has to take action, it is taking action all the time anyway, and it is the mind that is governing it. So change cannot merely be accomplished in the mind. But since the body's actions are dependent upon the mind's instructions, then change must first be accomplished in the mind. Deepak Chopra's work (1996) has also shown how healthy minds produce healthy bodies.

'Our life is what our thoughts make it.'
Dale Carnegie

There has been increasing evidence of the kind of 'mind over matter' that these thinkers and writers have suggested for decades – if not centuries. One example is the kind of work that has been conducted by Robert Jahn, Professor of Aerospace Science in his Princeton Engineering Anomalies Research laboratory. Subjects were able to influence the outcome of a random number generator so that it produced higher or lower number events than would be expected by chance. Jahn's view is that consciousness operates much as quantum mechanics does at the sub-atomic level, and this is certainly in accord with Deepak Chopra's perspective on the quantum aspects of human mental processes. If it can work with machines there is no reason why it should not work on our bodies (see Jahn and Dunne 1987; Jahn 1996).

I used to be very much of a rationalist until I came across the Transcendentalist movement and the works of Ralph Waldo Emerson and Henry David Thoreau who had established their ideas in the 1830s. The Transcendentalists were in part reacting to 18th-century rationalism, and partly rejecting elements of their Puritan heritage. What they were mostly opposed to was religious ritualism and dogmatic theology. The Transcendentalists were influenced by aspects of romanticism, such as self-examination and the celebration of individualism. They extolled the virtues of nature. Intuition was favoured over reason since they believed that the divinity of the universe permeated all things and formed a direct correspondence with the individual soul. They saw the surrounding natural world as containing both beauty and truth.

For some people this represents quite a leap of faith. But my conviction in the power of mind and spirit has been restored regularly. I once participated in a 'remote viewing' experiment in which more than 200 people were asked to think of one of four photographic images that were concealed from them but known to the presenter. He told us that he was thinking about image 'A' and he asked the audience to draw quick sketches of that image. More than 60% of the audience sketched something that had similarities to image 'A' when the pictures were revealed. Of course the presenter had seen all the four images and what interested me most was that the rest of us all drew something that had similarities to one of the other images. Now I don't know if this is telepathy and it doesn't really matter. What does matter is that the human mind, spirit, brain or soul is capable of much more than our materialistic rational thought expects.

WAY 13 Feeling the fear, and not doing it anyway

'Lessen your fear because if you let it grow it is you who will become small.'
Amazonian oral tradition

It is important to get the balance right between courage and caution. Every time you 'feel the fear' you do not have to 'do it anyway' (despite Susan Jeffers' exhortation). There are times when you might be fearful but simply do 'have' to act. But there are other times when you are fearful and feel that you 'ought' to act. Making the choice between courage and caution depends on context: just how important is it, on this occasion, that you do something even though you don't really want to?

When I was very young my elder sister tried to encourage me to join a tennis club. She thought it would be good for me. I resisted with a range of excuses but really I was afraid of the unknown, of meeting new people and a new situation and not knowing how to 'be'. I persuaded a friend to join with me and was so glad that we both gained new friends, a life-long love of the game and the ability to learn how to build up the courage to enter each new situation.

It is certainly true that fear is the real enemy: '...fear of lack, fear of failure, fear of sickness, fear of loss and feeling of insecurity on some plane' (Scovel-Shinn 1925: 13). These fears act on the subconscious and can bring about the very thing that is feared. I learned that lesson when I was attempting high diving. My fear got in the way of technique and as a result I executed a spectacular bellyflop, hurt myself and never tried high diving again. The point is:

I didn't need to. There was no need to risk another humiliation, quite apart from the pain. I had no plans for a diving career. Interestingly my diving companions, who were successful in their learning, carried on diving, but never made fun of me for not continuing to try.

'Courage is resistance to fear, mastery of fear – not absence of fear.'
Mark Twain

Clearly there will be some things you need to try to accomplish, even with the element of fear. But choose those actions with care and make sure you are not doing it for someone else's benefit. Only 'do it anyway' for your own benefit.

You may have already heard of the 'fight/flight' mechanism. When you experience something you fear, you should think about how this mechanism works. It is perfectly natural for human beings to fear some things – it is a self-protection system that we hold in common with all animals. Animals instinctively fear predators and even though humans have less to fear in the natural environment there is still a relic of these instinctive fears in all of us, even in the so-called 'civilised' world. The interesting thing is how those fears vary between individuals: some are afraid of snakes or spiders, others of open spaces and yet others of closed, confined spaces.

As with all animals we have to make rapid choices of whether to fight in the face of our fears or run away as fast as we can. The problem for humans is that we cannot fight all the things we fear – even if we have the physical strength – nor can we run away from some of our fears.

A good example of this can be found in some of the more common 'fears' – like speaking in public, attending a job interview, or sitting an exam.

When we encounter something we fear, our mind and body together quickly produce a set of very natural physiological responses. Our heart will beat more rapidly, we breathe too fast and not deeply enough, we have 'butterflies' in the stomach, feel nervous or nauseous and may need the toilet. The main muscle that runs through the 'core' of our body – the psoas – activates to keep us ready to run or fight. Sometimes it goes into spasm and that makes it hard for us to relax again. Once more these are all natural responses in that the body is preparing us either to run or to fight – we will need to elevate our pulse, to increase blood flow, get more oxygen to the brain and muscles,

empty our stomach and bowels and so on.

What I have just described is experienced by many as a 'panic attack'. Indeed just by describing this, and perhaps even by mentioning something you may fear, you may have started to experience some of these sensations in a mild form. For some people the fear of having a panic attack can become generalised and may be worse than the actual attack itself. Any emotion, experience or memory that triggers the same physical sensation reminds them of their previous anxiety. Even if I only *think* about an unpleasant exam experience all those physical sensations come back to me again in a milder form.

But think about how quickly these responses occur. They are almost automatic. And – *this is very important* – if they can arise quickly, they can also subside quickly. The trick is to help the mind and the body to return to its more relaxed, stable state.

> **TIP:** There are several ways to deal with these sensitised responses to anticipated anxieties or concerns. You can even use these to help someone else having a panic attack.
>
> To prevent hyperventilation, close your mouth and breathe through the nose for a while.
>
> If your anxiety increases... count three while taking in a breath through your nose, hold for three and exhale from your mouth for three. Continue until anxiety subsides.

It is almost impossible to laugh and experience anxiety. So if you can find something to laugh about anxiety will be inhibited.

If you sense anxious feelings developing then, in your mind, 'shout' STOP! ... and thereby interrupt the catastrophic thought.

Try even 'seeing' in your mind's eye a big road sign saying STOP!

Then give yourself some coping statements such as:
'These feelings will pass in three minutes.'
'I cannot die from this feeling.'
'I will not faint.'

Or if you have specific fears:
'I am much bigger than a spider, it cannot hurt me.'
'Air travel is one of the safest forms of travel.'

1 2 3 4 5 6 7 8
9 10 11 12 13 **14**
15 16 17 18 19
20 21 22 23 24
25 26 27 28 29
30 31 32 33 34
35 36 37 38 39
40 41 42 43 44
45 46 47 48 49

Chapter 5

THE DOMINANCE OF MIND AND SPIRIT

© depositphotos.com

'Beyond a wholesome discipline, be gentle with yourself.
You are a child of the universe no less than the trees and the stars;
you have a right to be here. And whether or not it is clear to you,
no doubt the universe is unfolding as it should.'

From Max Ehrmann's 'Desiderata'

WAY 14 Using the spirit

There are times when we feel that our bodies constrain or dominate us to the extent that we are limited in what we can accomplish. That occurs when we feel tired or fatigued or as in the 'fight/flight' syndrome mentioned above. The previous two chapters aimed to move us away from that view towards one in which the mind can be more in control. Limitations upon individual success due to the inadequacies of our body can be overcome mentally just as you can lessen the fight/flight anxieties. Thus the mind, spirit or soul (call it what you will) must be protected and cultivated.

This can be the same for people with physical disability. I have a friend who was born with a 'withered' arm: one arm did not grow and has little muscle function. Yet he goes skiing and mountain climbing and conducts guided mountain walking tours. His view is that he wasn't going to let his altered physical ability control how he lived his life. One could say his spirit challenged the limitations of his body. Others might say that he 'minded' (was bothered about) the limitations on what he could do and used that mental power to overcome the restrictions.

We assume that mental power is contained within the mind. And it is generally assumed that 'the mind' is contained within the brain. Often we assume that mental power depends upon our brain function. Yet the fact that the brain is contained within and physiologically dependent upon the body is one of the many paradoxes of human existence. The brain controls the body, while it cannot do that controlling without the support of the body.

This relationship between brain and body is reciprocal. You can have your body do something that will influence your brain/mind or have your mind/brain do something that will influence your body (Chopra 1996). Both popular beliefs and scientific ideas about this relationship have to reconcile the apparent contradictions of freedom and control. There are popular convictions about our individual fates based upon understandings of biology, astrology, biorhythms and so on, and yet the belief in action and personal development, and the belief in our own ability to control our survival endures.

Although the mind cannot be separated from the body people often behave as if they are separate. They do it either to help understand or analyse their mind and body: it is less complex than trying to make sense of them together. Deepak Chopra points out '... there is no real duality (of mind and body)... we have divided mind and body in the first place – so that we can understand the physiology.' (Chopra 1996: 65) The artificial duality of mind and body was a consequence of scientific analysis.

An additional complication is that we tend to sense bodily constraints more readily than we are aware of any constraints of the mind. Pain, fatigue, soreness are all immediately apparent, requiring us to act to lessen any discomfort. But mental 'errors' tend to hide themselves more easily and it can take us some time to realise they are taking place. Csikszentmihalyi's (1996, 1997) work on 'flow' implies that individual success depends upon a perfect symbiosis between mind and body. Success in a range of accomplishments from artistic to sporting to health performances depends upon complete absorption in the activity. Chopra's argument is that an intelligent sense of selfhood is the driving force towards health.

So while there is some need to understand the balance of power between the brain and the rest of the body, most of the evidence suggests that the mind dominates. Ultimately our mental power, our 'spirit', can greatly influence how our body 'performs'.

Bear in mind also that our perceptions and therefore our understanding of the world are mediated by our senses; and our senses in turn are governed by the structure of the brain and by the given nature of the material and social environment. So language and communication processes are central to that mediation. This is why I suggested earlier that storytelling is a key element in communication. In essence stories feed our mind. And, as we have shown, our mind, in turn, influences our body. Stories are groups of words that are structured in a particular manner. The following are just some of the physical effects that can be seen when telling stories.

Stories can:

- create physiological responses in the form of emotional display (e.g. blushing)
- raise or lower blood pressure
- send people to sleep
- increase adrenalin flow
- raise or lower body temperature
- increase immune response activity
- induce analgesia and anaesthesia.

Storytelling is one way in which the human spirit is stimulated. But there are others and they draw upon the religious, ethnic or cultural contexts in which we were brought up. This means that there are a variety of views on exactly what the human spirit is. We do not need to engage in that debate here – rather we need to acknowledge the existence of the spiritual and look at some suggested ways in which it can be harnessed.

Just consider the power of prayer. You may or may not at present use prayer. It might have become a thoughtless routine in a religious assembly, something you do 'religiously' every night, or something you might have rejected as having no rational basis. For me the most interesting thing I have discovered is that prayer can actually 'work'. I discovered the work of Dr Larry Dossey, a scientist/physician whose work has shown how powerful beliefs can be in the healing process (1991, 1993). After studying prayer using orthodox randomised controlled trial methods, the ones employed to test the efficacy of pharmaceutical drugs, he has shown that prayer can effectively heal – and even do that at a distance. In other words, something is going on, even if we do not know exactly what it is. This is both the problem and the prospect of the spiritual in our lives. But just because we cannot fully explain it does not mean we should rule it out. Whoever or whatever you can envisage as your 'guiding spirit', pray to them: it is worth trying. In some respects it resembles meditation, but instead of emptying your mind you need to be precise in what you ask for when you pray. It helps in clarifying your goals.

Another neglected powerful spiritual source is music:

'What is this magical medium that moves, enchants, energizes, and heals us? In an instant, music can uplift our soul. It awakens within us the spirit of prayer, compassion, and love. It clears our minds and has been known to make us smarter ...It is the primal breath of creation itself, the speech of angels and atoms, the stuff of which life and dreams, souls and stars, are ultimately fashioned.'

Don Campbell

While we often use music to entertain, we fail to see its full potential in supporting our well-being. Music affects us emotionally, psychologically, intellectually and physically. It operates upon us directly in a neurophysiological way influencing our visual, auditory and kinesthetic patterns. Don Campbell's (1991) work has shown these effects very clearly and, in particular, he emphasises the value of Mozart's music which can create a profound sense of order and clarity without being overly sentimental. I have already cautioned about your choice of music but I too find one can't go far wrong with Mozart.

Try this

Music has been 'exploited' as a background to try to guide people's behaviour. You find it in factories to encourage people to work steadily or in shops to get people to buy things. You find it in hotels and shopping malls to create a certain mood – again probably to encourage you to spend money. So this is something you need to guide for yourself: note how many more people resist the pressure of others' sounds by 'plugging in' to their own MP3 players.

You will need to experiment with finding pieces of music that calm, uplift and restore you; ones that make you happy or that inspire you. I suggest trying classical music or at least music without words – that way the music becomes what you wish it to be. You can interpret it for your own needs.

The one piece that works every time for me is the second movement of Mozart's Concerto for Clarinet. You will recognise it. I find it calming, peaceful and inspiring – it actually makes me breathe more easily!

'The heart of man has been so constituted by the Almighty, that like a flint, it contains a hidden fire which is evoked by music and harmony, and renders man beside himself with ecstasy. These harmonies are echoes of that higher world of beauty which we call the world of spirits; they remind man of his relationship to that world, and produce in him an emotion so deep and strange that he himself is powerless to explain it.'

Al-Ghazzali

WAY 15 Practical intuition

As you can guess from the previous Way, I am leading on to asking you to suspend your ability to 'reason' and begin to get in tune with your intuition. Some of us have very powerful intuitive experiences. Others may have them without realising it. If the latter applies to you I advise that you may be missing an opportunity. So this Way is to encourage you to develop your intuitive abilities: they may have some practical advantages.

Let me explain by telling you about something that happened to me. In the late 1980s I experienced several episodes of an intuitive nature that on at least a couple of occasions might have saved my life. On one occasion in 1991 my wife and I were visiting friends in Milwaukee, Wisconsin, and went in to a second-hand bookshop. As usual she went off to look at the sections that interest her and I perused my areas of interest. It was an enormous shop with the books stacked high. It was quiet and there seemed to be no one else there. My wife was a couple of stacks away from me. I appeared to be alone. I was looking directly at the spines of the books in my section when the image of a large hunting knife appeared before my eyes – it was literally a 'vision'. The image prompted thoughts of danger so I immediately found my wife and told her we should leave right away. She had grown accustomed to heeding my 'intuitions', asked no questions and we left. As we were walking back towards a covered car park across some open ground she whispered to me that she thought we were being followed. As a ruse we turned around quickly and she pointed at some buildings with interest – as tourists do – and sure enough

there was a blond-haired man walking a short distance behind us carrying what looked like a second-hand paperback. We got a good look at him, although he did not look directly at us, even deliberately appeared to avert his eyes, and walked on by into the car park. We delayed heading back to the car but when we got there he was nowhere to be seen. A couple of months later, back in the UK, I caught an item on television news – the sound was not on but I recognised the images of the arrest of a blond-haired man: the one who followed us from the car park. I turned on the sound. He was dubbed 'The Milwaukee Mass Murderer'. My wife came back from the shops with a copy of the newspaper and, quite independently, she said: 'Look at the front page – isn't that the man who...?' etc. It was indeed Jeffrey Dahmer.

Now I certainly didn't fit his usual victim profile but he might have thought I was alone in the shop. That isn't the point. It was the stark image of the knife that prompted our departure from the shop. And I certainly hope that I can equally respond to any intuitive 'guidance' I receive that protects me and my loved ones in future. My father told me that my grandfather, who was a mariner, had decided not to go on a final transatlantic voyage due to a 'feeling' he had. The ship he was due to sail on was lost with all hands.

Evidently incidents such as these are likely to be, one hopes, quite rare. But there are plenty of opportunities for bringing intuition into our lives on a smaller scale that might help us pull ourselves together in a positive manner.

'Intuition is a spiritual faculty and does not explain, but simply points the way.'
Florence Scovel-Shinn

In some respects we do not need to explain how intuition works. It is best to simply make use of it and develop it. I encourage you to spend more time on sources of intuition.

Our most familiar intuitions occur in dreams and often it can help to analyse or interpret a dream for how it might be trying to help us solve a problem or deal with difficult situations, or offer some insights into dealing with your life. Unless you can find a skilled dream analyst, the best way to do this yourself is to write down all you can remember from a dream – even the smallest details. And then read it again a day or two later. Often that is when it makes more sense or offers an unforeseen insight. Meditation is another way to open up further intuitive resources. It works because it allows us to temporarily sidestep the conscious mind with its rational impulse to always do things 'logically'.

But I also suggest doing some practical intuition exercises of the kind recommended by Laura Day http://www.practicalintuition.com/. Intuition is an internal, subconscious mechanism that can help with our life decisions. You might call it 'instinct' or a 'gut feeling' that can be so pressing you need to respond to it somehow. Laura Day defines it as '...a nonlinear, non-empirical process of gaining and interpreting information in response to questions.' (Day 1996: 83) She is quite rigorous about ensuring that the questions you are seeking an answer to are not ambiguous: they should be quite precise or the answers will not be clear. Also she points out that the impressions you receive don't have to make immediate sense to you, and often they appear in metaphorical form. Her point is that we all possess some intuitive ability to varying degrees, it just needs to be 'woken up' and developed.

This is an exercise to help you begin experimenting with your intuition.

Have a clear question in mind:

'If I take the job I have been offered, will it bring the rewards I am seeking?'

'If I marry this person will we both have the happiness we are seeking in our marriage?'

Try this

It helps if you either have an associate to listen to you and make notes, or failing that turn on an audio/tape recorder to record your impressions and sensations.

Close your eyes and notice your breathing for a minute or so. Then notice any physical sensations. Be aware of what they are and describe them out loud. Or notice if any sounds appear to you. Then, eyes still closed, look into the darkness. Describe any colours, or images that emerge. Be patient. There may be colours, or shapes. They may be blurry or symbolic or quite clear and defined. Let whatever comes, come.

Allow yourself 15 to 20 minutes for this exercise. Keep the recording of your images, or the notes from your associate and look at them later. They might not make sense right away but possibly they will later.

I did this once and the images that came to me were of a 19th century scene with horses and carriages in a snowy landscape with trees. My wife recorded the notes of my images. We were in the UK at the time with no plans for travel. In a week or so I received an invitation to speak at a conference in Montreal. I planned that we could visit friends in Chicago, hire a car and drive to Montreal after seeing them. As we arrived at our friends' place, they put us up in a house they had only recently bought. As we entered the bedroom my wife and I saw the antique pictures on the wall – snow scenes with horses and carriages in a forest. Our friends had bought the pictures from an antique shop about the time we were conducting the intuition experiment.

Try this

An interesting experiment to try is the following, which will be done with one or more persons who will serve as your reader(s):

To begin, you will supply answers to questions that neither you nor the reader knows. Write questions secretly (say about ten each) on separate but identical pieces of paper. Put each question in an envelope. Neither you nor the other person looks at it yet.

Tell your reader that each envelope contains a question, which they will not see, and you would like them to report the impressions they receive. Tell them that if they receive nothing, just make something up. Don't tell them they will be doing a reading, or even that they will be answering the questions you wrote down.

Hand each reader an envelope, still closed, have them report their impressions. Note what they say. (Probably it is best to write them down for accuracy.) After they have done this, open the envelope and see how the things they reported apply to the question you asked. You will most likely be very surprised to find out how accurately the question(s) were answered.

Trust your intuition. Either act in response to an urgent impression, or write down the 'messages' you receive since some of the symbols and metaphors will only make sense later.

1 2 3 4 5 6 7 8
9 10 11 12 13 14
15 **16 17 18 19**
20 21 22 23 24
25 26 27 28 29
30 31 32 33 34
35 36 37 38 39
40 41 42 43 44
45 46 47 48 49

Chapter 6

MAINTAINING A HEALTHY BODY

'Physical fitness is
not only one of the
most important keys
to a healthy body, it is
the basis of dynamic
and creative
intellectual activity.'

John F. Kennedy

© depositphotos.com

WAY 16 Health rules

None of the advice given in the rest of this book will work if your body does not provide the physical foundation for your personal goals. A healthy body enables you to focus on the rest of your life. The problem is that we do tend to take our body for granted and only question our health when it is disturbed by illness.

> **'Personal responsibility, self-value and high regard and reverence for life are the primary determinants of health.'**
> *Edward A. Taub*

One element of taking control of your own life requires taking responsibility for your own health. Once again this does not rule out taking advantage of whatever expert professional help is available. But the foundations are up to you. My approach to the foundations for a healthy body follows principles of 'natural hygiene'. Harvey and Marilyn Diamond wrote a very comprehensive book explaining these principles called *Fit For Life* (1985). The idea is that, if treated properly and barring accidents, the body is quite good at maintaining itself.

It is best to begin by thinking about food and diet. Too often people think of a diet as about eliminating certain foodstuffs in order to 'lose weight'. But your 'diet' is not only about what you *don't* eat, it is more about what you *do* eat. Nutrition, like physical exercise, is vital (i.e. 'necessary for life') and so getting your diet right should be an obvious focus of concern. Again you should have a look at Martina Watts' excellent book *49 Ways to Eat Yourself Well* (2013) that goes into much more detail about food and diet.

Proper treatment of the body requires ingesting the right kinds of nutrients in the right way. In essence, we need enzymes to digest food properly and ensure the body has access to nutrients, and we need to avoid the toxins that damage our physiology.

TIP: The principles are quite simple...

Avoid over-processed, refined food.
Maintain high water content in your food intake.
Attend to the acid/alkaline balance of foods.
Avoid artificial or known 'problematic' ingredients.
Seek out fresh, organic, natural foods by preference.
Ensure a balance between raw and cooked foods.

As an illustration take the eating of fruit. Most people know fruit is good for you ('An apple a day...' etc.). But which fruits and when to eat them is rarely thought about. The first thing to remember is that fruit is digested very quickly, much quicker than any other food. It is best to eat fruit on its own and not, as is traditional, just after a meal. If you eat it as a dessert it will help push through everything else you have just eaten – most of which would normally take hours to digest. (And if you eat meat it will take much longer to digest.) If the fruit is 'rushing' your digestion you will not get the nutrition you desire from the food you have just eaten. So eat fruit before a meal as a 'starter', since most fruits are digested within 20 minutes.

When I was playing competitive squash I realised that I had put on some weight and players I should have beaten were beginning to beat me since I tired early and was carrying too much body weight. So I tried the 24-hour fruit fast that I read about in the Diamonds' *Fit For Life* book. Once a week I would only eat fruit for 24 hours. It meant carrying a lot of apples and bananas around with me and drinking lots of water too. You are supposed to make sure you don't get hungry so eating the fruit throughout the day, not just at mealtimes, was essential. I lost the unnecessary extra weight I was carrying quite quickly and felt better for it – as well as starting to win at squash again.

These natural hygiene principles originate from the idea of 'food combining' and what became known as the the 'Hay Diet'. In the 1920s Dr William Howard Hay noted how humans tend to eat much more complex diets and food combinations than any other creatures. More so now globalisation leads us to expect similar foods to be available all year round. We put them together in rich cultural combinations: Tex-Mex, Italian, French, Indian, Balti, and Japanese. Such food variety can be found in restaurants and in supermarkets in most fair sized towns.

Dr. Hay pointed out how foods combine when ingested is crucial to understanding how the body assimilates and eliminates them. Food which is incompletely digested is difficult to eliminate. If what is not required to power the body is not eliminated then the body becomes toxified by this excess and gains weight. Hay applied these principles to his 'cures' which he attributed to taking foods in a natural form and not mixing proteins and starches at the same meal. (Ivan Pavlov's experiments with dogs showed that starches are digested in about two hours, proteins are digested in about four hours but a protein/starch mixture can still be digesting 13 hours later. Food taken on top can lead to fermentation and toxic by-products putting strain on the whole physiological system.)

There are some simple examples: as a vegetarian if I eat an omelette it should be with a salad, not with potatoes. If you eat steak, again, take it with a salad not with chips (French fries). If you want chips, then have them with a salad. (See http://www.synergy-health.co.uk/home/h-p/the-hay-diet/. Also see Le Tissier 1992; Grant and Joice 1984)

But there are other times when we can take very straightforward care of what we eat. I had a colleague who was concerned about putting on too much weight. She was a health professional and so was well aware of what she should and shouldn't eat, so I asked her what in particular concerned her. It was that she could eat a whole packet of chocolate biscuits in one sitting. Of course she knew she shouldn't. But she 'couldn't stop herself'. It didn't take long to identify the problem: she would come home from a hard day's work, sit down to watch her favourite soap opera on TV with a cup of tea – and a packet of biscuits. So she wasn't really focused on the eating, the TV took up all her concentration and she didn't really 'notice' eating all those biscuits.

If you find yourself indulging in more 'treats' than you know you should:

Try this

1) If you suffer from the same 'problem' that my colleague experienced – when you sit down ready to watch the TV take only two biscuits from the packet, put them on a plate and then... put the packet back in the cupboard!

2) Whenever you 'treat' yourself with food, biscuits or chocolate or whatever, then you must allow time to fully appreciate that indulgence. Thus I have chocolate every day – but it is one square of the best quality, organic dark chocolate with high cocoa content and I make sure that I fully notice the taste sensations that chocolate gives me. I do nothing else when I am 'noticing' that taste. (Chocolate taken in that way is very good for you – honestly!)

Generally it is best for your digestion only to focus on the food itself. Avoid reading or watching television when eating. Notice the taste and texture of food and enjoy it.

Fluid intake can be another area of ignorance. Water is the main constituent of the human body. It is equal to 75% of body weight. The brain is 75% water. Most people do not drink enough water. Most are suffering from chronic, low-level dehydration. We should drink about 1.5 litres a day, quite apart from any other fluid intake, and that should be adjusted upwards for any extra dehydrating activities (such as sitting in front of a VDU, travel, driving, and exercise). The average loss of water from our body on a cool day is 1.6 litres (33.3% through the skin, 33.3% through the lungs and the rest from urine excretion). If the loss is not replenished the filtering capacity of the kidneys is reduced. Adequate water intake prevents constipation, lethargy and headaches, and is generally effective as part of the body's homeostasis and defence against disease.

We should therefore drink water even when we are not thirsty. Edmund Hillary's conquest of Everest was in part due to his doctor's realisation that the previous (Swiss) team had failed and became exhausted since they only consumed two glasses of water a day. He insisted they took in 12 glasses and provided special snow heating devices to get the water.

In fact, the neglect of our body's need for rehydration is so great that we often even fail to recognise thirst any more and confuse it with hunger (see Batmanghelidj, 2000). Next time you feel hungry and are tempted to indulge in a big meal, drink a glass of water first. I once 'cured' a patient with water. He came to me because of regular and serious bouts of nausea, which he believed was psychological due to ongoing family crises. He thought hypnosis might help. I asked him about his daily routine and it became obvious he travelled a lot, worked in enclosed environments, drinking only coffee and alcohol throughout the day. He was clearly dehydrated. I taught him self-hypnosis to encourage him to drink a glass of water every hour or so – the problem was fixed. Of course, if he had remembered to drink the water every hour anyway he would not have needed the hypnosis.

Filter the water you wish to drink if it is sourced from the mains supply and when filtered water is not easily available drink mineral water.

Paying attention to what we ingest does not meaning ruling out all sources of food pleasure. We may have our 'drugs' of choice and they will not harm us if we extend the health rules to how we use them. Empowerment must extend to our bodies and control over our personal 'poisons'. Mine is coffee, and after having detoxified from coffee a few times, and going through great discomfort to do so, I drew up a set of rules that allows me my poison while doing the best not to poison myself.

TIP: Draw up your own rules for whatever you imbibe or ingest that you know might not always be good for you. You could substitute alcohol, cream cakes, sugary soft drinks and so on for the coffee rules below.

Coffee Rules

1) It is not necessary to have a cup of coffee every day.

2) Only take a cup of coffee when there is enough time to fully enjoy the experience.

3) Drinking coffee must be a pleasant (romantic, aesthetic and sensual) experience in terms of location, time and company.

4) Only drink cups of coffee that demonstrate quality in terms of it being well made: good taste, high quality, and excellent (e.g. organic) ingredients.

5) Take only two small cups of good quality coffee on any single day.

6) Compromise with these rules must be rare.

WAY 17 Leisure and rest

'If you intend to procrastinate, do it now!'

If you are tired, then rest. If you are 'too tired' to do anything then go to bed, and sleep. Don't exhaust yourself or waste your time being seduced by the monotony of television; that is not relaxing. I had the privilege of coming across the Spanish 'siesta' in the late 1960s and what a revelation it was. We were visiting friends in central Spain, had a leisurely lunch and afterwards it was simply assumed we would all get comfortable and take a 15-minute nap in the lounge. The shutters were closed, we stopped talking, and slept. I found that really restorative and was able to enjoy the rest of an active and energetic day.

Japanese businessmen later turned that into the 'power nap' and even invented a chair for doing it in. But the principle is the same. To rest and sleep after lunch is to do what is really a natural need of our body's circadian (daily) rhythm. All too often the pressures of modern life prevent us from doing that, but if you can and when you can, give it a try. Don't sleep for too long since that upsets your biorhythm and can interfere with night-time sleep.

You also need to think about how to incorporate 'rest' periods into your work schedule. There is plenty of evidence to show that there is a time limit to how effective we can be when working. Think about when you are doing an intense physical labouring task, inevitably your muscles weaken after a length of time so you need to take rest. The same is true of mental work. I know that I can only write effectively for two to three hours at a time. If I push myself and stay at the desk longer my thinking slows and so does my writing. So I have learned to stop after a few hours and go and do something completely different. It could be working in the garden for an hour or going for a walk. What matters is that it is a genuine break from the work; the mind can rest, and so can the body. Again, such a break can be restorative and you will work more effectively when you return to your desk. If your work is more physical in nature then your break time could involve reading or writing and thinking instead.

It is surprising how hard it is for some people to follow this principle. Ironically, we can get into a workplace comfort zone that keeps us driving at things, accomplishing tasks, meeting deadlines, and we stay in the comfort zone because we are used to it – not because we are genuinely 'comfortable'. Such a zone can be demanding, oppressive and tiring. So we might have to consider mindfully changing our comfort zone and finding the zone that really is comfortable – one that is in accord with the true rhythm of our physiology and psychology.

TIP: Take breaks from work, no matter how short. (If people are allowed to take a break to go outside for a smoke, then you are perfectly entitled to break for a drink of water or to step outside for a breath of fresh air.)

Switch tasks.

Sometimes it helps to have two or three tasks running in parallel so that if you find yourself becoming less effective in one task you can switch to another. That way your mental approach can be revitalised and you will be more effective when you return to the original task.

Often we face deadlines and cannot simply switch tasks no matter how boring one task has become. If I am reading a lengthy report that I have to comment on, I use the 'Do Five More' rule. Thus I will read the report in stages and to get through a difficult patch I say to myself: 'OK, just read five more pages and then take a break'. If I know I only have to read five more pages and then allow myself a change it is surprising how effectively I can read those five pages. So turning the task into do-able 'chunks' improves my performance. I am in effect giving myself realistic deadlines which will eventually produce a reading of the full report.

It is important to remain alert to our body's and our mind's need for rest. And sometimes even the most eminent experts forget how to do this. I used to attend a regular committee meeting with medical colleagues in a well-appointed room in a hospital with air conditioning. There were surgeons, consultants, anaesthetists, nursing staff and so on. On one occasion we all appeared 'below par' and fortunately a clinical pathologist colleague, who was a particularly astute analyst, noticed that discussion had dulled, we appeared a little soporific and some of us had bloodshot eyes.

He immediately identified a lack of oxygen and took the restorative step of opening a window. The improvement was immediate; we breathed fresh air and restored our energy for the meeting.

Some people restore themselves by going on a retreat, playing their regular game of tennis, rowing on the river or walking in a park. They come back to an altered comfort zone. When we lived in the city of Chester in the UK my wife and I would prepare for the day with a brisk walk around the Roman walls of the town and we met plenty of other 'regulars' who walked or ran the walls every morning.

WAY 18 Appropriate activity

Some physical activity is essential to keep your body in good 'running order'. But that activity must be appropriate to your abilities, interests and needs. For example: I find playing tennis more enjoyable than rugby, and it is not just about avoiding 'rough and tumble', it has more to do with the rhythm of the game and the sound of the ball on the racquet.

You might never have enjoyed physical exercise but there are always some basic activities that do not require particular skills, or do not have to be performed in public, but which can have profound value for your physical health.

Walking is one such example. Frédéric Gros (2014) has written inspirationally about the value of walking. It is one of the easiest and most natural forms of physical exercise since you only have to put one foot in front of the other and start moving forward. No extra equipment is required. While walking we 'inhabit' the landscape, dwell in it and absorb it as we are moving. Philosophers, poets and political activists have all gained insight and responses from walking: think of Friedrich Nietzsche, William Wordsworth, Henry Thoreau, and Mahatma Gandhi. Walking's rhythmic monotony engages you with gravity, keeping you in contact with the earth, while allowing gentle contemplation, even perhaps a semi-meditative state which can clear the mind, exercising both your thoughts and your cardiovascular and lymphatic system at the same time. A 20-minute walk each day could be enough to offer such rewards, but remember to do it steadily and mindfully.

From Thoreau: A traveller asked Wordsworth's servant to show him her master's study; she answered: "Here is his library, but his study is out of doors."

Whatever activity you choose it helps to make it a regular part of your daily routines. Thus some exercises are best in the morning and some in the evening. You have to 'design' your day to suit your circumstances. But the routine reminds you to take the exercise and how best to perform it. All your physical exercise, like your mental exercise, should be performed mindfully, slowly, and with control. You need to engage in a balanced amount of cardiovascular (energetic) activity and simple stretching activities (to warm and activate muscles and lymphatic flow).

As with everything else I am advising in this book it is important you take your time and reflect upon my suggestions. Too often those I love and care for have chosen not to take useful advice; not just from me. I have witnessed great resistance from many people. When I coached squash it was alarming how often players did not do the simple warm-up/cool-down routine that I taught them before and after a pretty intensive contest; and then they wondered why they sustained muscle injuries or were pretty sore the following day.

The models for my recommended physical activities are Pilates, yoga and the Alexander Technique. The exercises I suggest are in the 'Try this' section on page 76, but throughout these exercises there are two basic instructions that improve their effectiveness:

A) Breathing:

You'd be surprised how people forget to breathe or breathe incorrectly during exercise. Remember to breathe in deeply through the nose and exhale slowly through the mouth. Occasionally allow low-abdominal breathing – not always from the chest. Drop breathing down to the abdomen. Expand abdominal muscles to inhale, contract to exhale.

B) Core muscle control:

Your core muscles are to be found behind your 'six-pack' – behind those front abdominals. You can activate them adequately by drawing in your stomach area as fully as you can and then releasing it to about halfway back to its starting position. Then hold it there whenever you are exercising and especially when lifting things. This is known as 'getting your connection'.

Have a look at *49 Ways to Move Yourself Well* (2015) by Andrew Bellamy who provides more ideas for breathing and developing core strength, as well as exploring movement in much more detail. In the meantime, while being mindful about breathing and core muscle control, try the following exercises, each of which will only take up about 10 minutes of your daily time.

Try this every morning, it will only take about ten minutes in all:

1) A simple roll-down:

Stand upright with your knees slightly bent and your arms limp at your side. Get your core muscle connection as instructed earlier. Take a breath in and, as you breathe out, gently roll down forward towards your toes. Let your head drop gently and let your arms remain loose and drop down too. Do not go beyond your comfortable point, at which you can feel a little stretching. At your lowest point, take a breath in and, while breathing out, roll back up again slowly. Do this three times. My excellent Pilates coach used to advise imagining rolling down 'one vertebra at a time' and then, when rolling back up, 're-stacking the vertebrae one at a time'. (There was once a time I could not touch my toes but after practising this exercise I can now do it every time.)

2) Gentle neck stretches:

Take a breath and as you breathe out slowly tilt your head to your left. Don't stretch too far, just to a comfortable position so that you can feel the stretch. Take a breath in and slowly return your head to the central position. Do the same again two more times. Then repeat the head tilt three times to your right. Next take the breath in, and then turn your head slowly to your left. At your furthest comfortable point, breathe in and repeat the exercise three times to your right. To finish this stage, breathe in and bow your head slowly forward to its furthest comfortable point, feeling the stretch. Then breathe in and slowly return to the central position. Again, do it two more times and then repeat the exercise, tilting your head slowly backwards and remembering to breathe throughout.

3) Gentle neck rolls:

After doing the previous gentle stretching activities, you can do some easy neck rolls. Take a breath and gently bow your head forward and roll it slowly around clockwise three times, breathing steadily as you go. Then repeat this in an anti-clockwise direction. (I often hear some interesting 'crunching' noises from my vertebrae when doing this – but don't be alarmed, it shows that such flexibility is required.)

4) Shoulders 'down':

Place your arms at your sides with your palms facing inward to your thighs. Keeping your arms to the side of your body slowly turn your hands out away from the side of your body, leading with your thumbs. Take a breath in and as you slowly release it, raise your arms up to and over your head so that your palms eventually come together over your head. Do not raise your shoulders while doing this. (You might not be able to have your palms meet at the top at first, eventually you will be able to.) At your highest point, breathe in and lower your arms to your side again, repeating the exercise another two times.

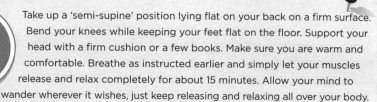

Try this

Try this every evening:

Take up a 'semi-supine' position lying flat on your back on a firm surface. Bend your knees while keeping your feet flat on the floor. Support your head with a firm cushion or a few books. Make sure you are warm and comfortable. Breathe as instructed earlier and simply let your muscles release and relax completely for about 15 minutes. Allow your mind to wander wherever it wishes, just keep releasing and relaxing all over your body.

Of course there are also plenty of cardio-vascular exercises that can improve your physical well-being on a regular basis. We've mentioned walking already. Walking at a steady pace for 20 minutes daily is excellent for your cardiovascular system. Cycling in a safe environment with the correct protective clothing is good too. Swimming is equally valuable – especially if you can avoid chlorine pools. A surprisingly effective exercise is a PT bouncer, which is like a mini-trampoline. With those you can even bounce to your favourite music. (Be careful not to bounce too much at first. Build it up slowly. More than a minute can be too much if you are not used to it.)

Since you are taking responsibility for your own progress, I assume you will not just take my word for what constitutes the best exercise for you. You will be starting to do your own research and compiling the evidence for what works in your case. Let me suggest the following analytic framework for anything you choose to do to improve your physical health.

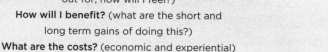

Ask these questions of anything suggested:

How do I do it? (the proposed methods and means)
Why do it? (an explanation of why and how it 'works')
What will I experience? (what symptoms to look out for; how will I feel?)
How will I benefit? (what are the short and long term gains of doing this?)
What are the costs? (economic and experiential)
What evidence is there for all the above? (what does the research say?)

You can test these questions against the exercises I have suggested above. Basically, I have told you how to do them. They are designed to improve your breathing, increase lymphatic and blood flow, and increase muscle flexibility. They do not require costly equipment and do not take up a great deal of time, considering the benefits. These include improved eyesight and brain function and reduced muscle soreness. Obviously you can do further research yourself for additional evidence, but the most telling evidence is how *you* feel and if you personally experience improved long term health.

The classic negative response to taking control of our own health is: 'Why go to so much trouble? You could get hit by a bus tomorrow!' So why bother? This is like inviting the bus to come along and hit you. These suggestions are simple and not particularly demanding, but the results will speak for themselves. My brother once challenged me about my concern for health. He asked: 'Do you want to live forever?' I said, 'No, I don't expect that, but I do want to live well'. It is not about not dying – nobody can solve that problem. It is all about *how* you live and how well you live. When people ask: 'Why bother – it is so complicated?' my reply

is: 'I'd rather pay attention to my good health than have to worry about bad health.' Prevention is always better than having to seek a cure.

I found the best explanation for the human being's place in nature and for living healthily in the world in Paungger and Poppe's *Moon Time* (1995): 'Not for a moment is Man a foreign body on the earth and in the universe. Nature is not engaged in any struggle with humanity but rather gives it everything it needs, as long as each individual learns to live in friendship with himself and with nature. This friendship can never be one that is prescribed by law. It is your own personal achievement, your own personal decision. The choice is always yours, no matter how hard people try to persuade you to the contrary.'

WAY 19

Too many plates in the air

'Simplicity is the ultimate sophistication.'
Leonardo da Vinci

If you don't get on top of things, they can soon get on top of you. So keep things as simple as you can.

Remember that circus or variety act when the juggler starts plates spinning on canes and then has to keep them all going, starting up more and more plates until the stage is full and he keeps spinning? 'Failure' occurs when a plate stops spinning and smashes to the ground.

I spent a great deal of my working life 'spinning plates'. I had to look at all my spinning plates and ask 'What are they all for?'. The best advice I can give you now as a consequence of my experience is: Don't try to keep *all* the plates spinning. Choose the most important ones, those you *must* keep spinning, and don't start spinning plates that aren't important or can wait until the important ones have had their run.

Richard Bach would remind us not to try to do too many things when you are 'flying upside down'. As far as possible do one thing at a time. Don't take pride in 'multi-tasking'. Inevitably you can only give partial attention to each task.

Multi-tasking = multi-failure!

If you can, *finish* a project before starting another. I once had a colleague who was great at coming up with ideas and starting projects.

But he was poor at finishing them and 'delivering the goods'. Most people do want to see the goods delivered so always bear in mind the 'deliverables'. Draw on the earlier 'Ways' to define and refine your goals, and your means and methods for getting there. Eliminate distractions in the way we suggested earlier. So don't do e-mail and/or answer the phone while writing a report or doing something that requires deep thinking. Turn off the phone and ignore e-mails; do them both later at times specified by you and most suited to you.

In modern life we are very often struggling to create order out of chaos. The problem is that chaos is part of the natural order. As Nietzsche is often quoted as observing: 'Out of chaos... sometimes comes a dancing star.' So the trick is how to use chaos constructively, but then to move from chaos to a manageable order in your life.

1 2 3 4 5 6 7 8
9 10 11 12 13 14
15 16 17 18 19
20 21 22 23 24
25 26 27 28 29
30 31 32 33 34
35 36 37 38 39
40 41 42 43 44
45 46 47 48 49

Chapter 7

EMPOWERING YOURSELF

© depositphotos.com

'Pessimism
leads to
weakness;
optimism leads
to power.'

William James

WAY 20 Beware crazymakers

'Hell is other people.'
Jean-Paul Sartre

Even good friends can drive you crazy sometimes. Julia Cameron (1994) cautions us to watch out for crazymakers. The worst kinds of crazymakers are those that have no sense of *your* time, *your* agenda and the things that *you* need to attend to. Take those people who turn up at your house unannounced and assume you can attend to them right away and that you have nothing better to do. They don't even ask if you are busy. The same thing happens when people phone you, 'for a chat'. Now you may be the sort of person who loves people to just drop in or call unexpectedly. Well that's OK but remember that means you must sacrifice whatever else you planned to do. If that upsets your rhythm or sense of order then don't blame the crazymaker later on when things you needed to do haven't been finished.

More importantly don't you be the crazymaker to others; they might be too polite to tell you that while you might like to drop in, they don't, and they might not like other people doing it.

Caller ID really does help you to evade the phone call crazymaker. My wife lost a friend when she kept calling in at our house unannounced. My wife tried to explain that she had things she wanted to get on with but her friend got 'huffy' and said: 'So I need an appointment now?' My wife said: 'It's not like that, but I would prefer if you would please phone beforehand to see if I'm free.' Her friend didn't visit again.

If you drop in unannounced you are being inconsiderate of your host's timetable or agenda; you are only concerned with your own. Perhaps you are afraid your friend might ask you not to call in – well that's OK – they will consider you a better friend if you consider their needs above your own. So you might risk losing a friend. But what kind of friend is it who doesn't at least attempt to recognise your needs, your timetable, your agenda? If you want people to respect your agenda it is best not to disrespect theirs.

'When someone shows you who they are, believe them the first time.'
Maya Angelou

When phoning someone ask if they are not occupied and have the time to take your call. When deciding to visit someone phone beforehand to see if they are free.

Try this

Effective communication is the key to managing relationships with potential crazymakers. Virginia Satir noticed that at times of stress people tend to adopt one of five language strategies and accompanying non-verbal patterns of communication (such as gestures and demeanour). These are:

- BLAMING
- PLACATING
- DISTRACTING
- COMPUTING
- LEVELLING

The first two are fairly obvious. 'Distracting' changes the subject, avoids the topic of the discussion and changes the angle. 'Computing' sounds very reasonable, such as when someone says: 'I'm sure there's a good reason for the delay...'; but it does bury the strong emotions involved, such as irritation and impatience, so it can be seen as inauthentic. Levelling is the most balanced and measured response; it strives for honesty and openness: 'Let me level with you.'

The communication specialist Suzanne Haden Elgin (1989) points out that it is not always wise to simply match these patterns. If you blame a blamer, placate a placater and distract a distracter, then stress levels for both can escalate. At least 'computing a computer' will defer any confrontation and 'levelling' can help de-escalate a situation.

Elgin also has lots of useful advice for dealing with verbal attacks. She suggests that if you 'take the bait' in a verbal attack, you are participating in a self-reinforcing feedback loop. Instead, look for the attack that is hidden in the communication, respond directly to it and get the following message across: 'Don't try that with me – I'm not playing that game.'

By not playing their game you are being assertive and taking the wind out of their sails.

Others are never the problem. It is always about your attitude to them. I had salutary lessons in perceptions of others from a friend of mine who is an innkeeper. I asked him about problems with guests – expecting him to have plenty of tales to tell. He told me that although he had been in business for 15 years he had only ever lost two things. On one occasion a couple went away with the liquid soap from the bathroom. A few days later he received $2.00 in the post from the man who had packed the soap in error, thinking it belonged to his wife. The other item he lost was a small antique plaque on the wall. My friend said: 'I figured they must have thought they needed it more than we do.' Such charitable responses are rare, but heartwarmingly instructive.

The other story he told me was about having trouble with one guest who was being rude and abusive in the dining room in front of all the other guests; evidently trying to goad my friend into a response. My friend said to him: 'I am sorry, sir, I don't know how to respond to you because we have never had anybody like you stay at the Inn before.' The man instantly stopped his abusive behaviour and the other guests applauded. In some respects, then, my friend was both 'distracting' and 'levelling'.

A friend told me about being visited by a 'laid back' 18-year-old relative from the Caribbean. The youth was behaving just as youths do, going out to clubs, drinking and being sick and so on, and the man had had enough and went into his bedroom giving him a piece of his mind: 'losing his cool'. After he had left the youth's bedroom, he regretted how angry he had become and went back in to apologise:

'I'm sorry I got so angry – but you made me mad.' The youth replied: 'Hey man. I didn't make you mad, you did that for yourself.' That certainly is an example of 'levelling' – even if it could still make one 'mad'.

Incidents such as these are 'Eureka' moments. Something stands out from the background of routine, mundane events and changes your view of the world, of people, of yourself. But a 'Eureka' moment is useless unless you remember it. Such events must become part of your strategy for empowerment. Remember them, repeat them to others when appropriate, but most importantly, learn from them and allow them to guide your own actions.

Decide how best you wish to relate to other people. Sometimes it is easy to fall into the trap of holding other people in contempt for their attitudes and habits. It is essential that you do not mock their tastes and dispositions. We can get very attached to the 'songs' we sing. Other people's songs can mean a lot to them, even if they seem schmaltzy to you. There is no need to be embarrassed for them, or for your association with them. Their schmaltz is special to them, so yours can be special to you.

'... keep company only with people who uplift you, whose presence calls forth your best.'
Epictetus

WAY 21 Saying 'no'

If you are not enjoying something you need to find the way to stop doing it. You need to have the sense to know when to say 'yes', and build the strength to say 'no' when necessary. Knowing who you are and what your needs and wants are is the key to being able to say 'no' to requests that will prevent or obstruct your own progress.

Generally we avoid having to say 'no' since we believe it might make us unpopular and, as a rule, human beings like to be liked. Market researchers discovered many years ago that it is easier to get people to say 'yes' in response to a survey question than to get them to answer 'no'. Salespeople are particularly skilled at getting positive responses from people. They have to be in order to sell their products. The trick here is to build a repertoire of 'response strategies' which make it easier for you to resist the pressure to go along with another's proposal if it is not in your interests.

Try this

1) **Keep responses simple:**
   'Sorry, I can't this time.' Or 'I'm afraid I am busy then.' Resist the temptation to offer too much explanation. More details offer more opportunities for argument and some revealed detail which might provide leverage with which the other person might try to change your mind.

2) **If unsure, buy time:**
   'Let me think about it and then I'll get back to you.'
   'I can't answer right away. I need to think about it.'

3) **Keep control of your planned leisure or work time:**
   If you had decided to take a break, holiday, rest, do some work or even if you intend to do nothing then use the phrase: 'Sorry, I have plans.' It is nobody's business what you 'plan' to do and it would be quite rude of them to continue to ask.

4) **Have a policy rule:**
   By saying: 'I'm sorry, I make it a rule never to lend my... (car, power tools, lawnmower, guitar, keyboards) to anyone.' This establishes a general rule and makes the rejection less personal.

Ironically there is a lot of advice like: 'Don't be a nay-sayer.' So take care to understand that this is not a negative position to take. In fact by choosing when to say 'no' you will be avoiding the 'disease to please'. Being 'positive' does not mean saying 'yes' to everything. Deciding to say 'no' is not just a negative response; it can be a very positive one.

Saying 'no' is liberating. By saying 'no' to something you don't want to do you have left yourself with time for doing the things you really do want to do. But saying 'no' in this thoughtful conscious way is not 'nay-saying', which is a little understood phenomenon. Actually there are all sorts of nay-sayers who don't care about the damage they cause. And sometimes they do this in the interests of humour. There are some types of humour that rely on there being a victim – someone who can be humiliated – and it is a form of disdain.

I once experienced this from someone whom I admired and respected. When I was quite young this person once asked me if I knew the meaning of the word 'erudite'. At the time I was inadequately erudite to know the answer. But on his encouragement I looked it up and gave him the answer. His lesson to me was about expanding one's vocabulary in the interests of clarity in communication. It was ironic therefore when, decades later, in his company I mentioned that I found a certain person slightly 'cavalier' in their actions. I was astonished that he, accompanied by and 'egged on' by others present, then ridiculed the use of the term by asking if the person I described wore a large hat with a feather in it and had a goatee beard and laughed a lot (etc.). The 'joke' was to put me down for expanding my vocabulary – not to listen to the content of my point but rather to trivialise it by focusing on a choice of word. Perhaps it hurt more than it should; but it hurt because of who it came from.

Nay-sayers come in all shapes and sizes. They ridicule, oppose, undermine for all sorts of reasons – but rarely in the interests of those they are 'nay-saying'. It's like demolishing someone's house without thinking about where they are now going to live. Saying 'no' does not mean you are being a nay-sayer!

WAY 22 Being kind

'Liberty consists in the freedom to do all that does not harm others.'
A Declaration of the Rights of Man, article 3, Resistance to Tyranny, c.1700

Kindness is a behaviour generally understood as a concern for others. While it is seen as an altruistic virtue, helping others in need with no direct advantage to the helper, there is now plenty of evidence to show that acts of kindness reward the helper with the release of neurotransmitters responsible for feelings of contentment and relaxation. (See https://www.uniiverse.com/neuroscience.)

Altruism and empathy are as much a part of our human nature as are aggression and anger. These are all emotions and behaviour of which we are capable, that we have the potential to act on. What matters is the context, the social setting which encourages one or other of these behaviours and, most importantly, our own ability to choose how to behave and what to think and feel. That choice is the degree to which our actions and feelings are not 'determined' by forces 'beyond our control'. It is vital that we recognise who and what we are and who or what we can be. If we are truly mindful we are less likely to allow aggression to take us over, we can allow ourselves to 'feel' for the other person. '...caring and generosity are just as natural as selfishness and aggression.' (Kohn 1990)

We have to allow people to become what they want to be without imposing our own fixed expectations upon them. Be patient. Wait to find out what they want to be and then allow them to become that. Do that without allowing it to touch you. Make no judgements and offer no criticism. Allow all possibilities. Accept that is simply the way the world is.

Try this when giving advice:

Wait until asked: don't give advice unless it is sought.

Listen carefully to others.

Don't judge: accept the advice-seeker's view of the world.

Have compassion – not just sympathy.

Give information if you have it. Acknowledge when you don't.

Free up people to make their own effective choices.

'Life is not made up of great sacrifices and duties but of little things: in which smiles and kindness given habitually are what win and preserve the heart and secure comfort.
Sir Humphrey Davy

WAY 23 Showing appreciation

How you relate to others is vital in helping them know how to relate to you. Saying 'thank you' and paying a compliment are such simple, gracious and authentic devices for making someone feel good about themselves. Generally if you make them feel good about themselves they will reciprocate and want you to feel good about yourself.

I have a friend who is an excellent chef but he rarely gets invited to dinner since people feel intimidated by his professional expertise. More than that, when he comes to eat at my house, I can see him not just enjoying the food and the company but 'tasting' the product, assessing its texture and presentation and so on. He forgets that when he comes to eat with me he should behave as a 'guest' not a 'food critic'.

When invited to eat with someone, even if the food isn't to your taste or is not well made, you return a lot to your host by showing your appreciation of the effort that has been put into the preparation. A few well-chosen words of thanks are all that is necessary to reward your host. Gratitude is showing appreciation. Sayings, words and phrases, which 'give thanks' mean that there is something to appreciate. This technique is as old as the hills. Proverbs, mottos, and fables are all designed to achieve this. When you look around and see something beautiful – a tree, a leaf, a door, a window, a stone wall – the joy you feel is appreciation, a sound sense of gratitude. That can all start from a guru saying: 'Look around you... Is there just one small thing you can appreciate?' We do have a 'natural' core of appreciation: for some of us it might be the cosmos, the stars, the chemistry of life, or our parents. But showing your appreciation for others' efforts is tremendously empowering – to you as well as to them.

'It is the child's spirit, which we are most happy when we most recover; remaining wiser than children in our gratitude that we can still be pleased with a fair colour or a dancing light.'
John Ruskin

It is perhaps surprising that gratitude has to be taught. But that probably is due to the effects of nay-sayers teaching us to be excessively cautious about showing appreciation. It is always easier to criticise, less easy to offer positive solutions. It is risky to stick your head above the parapet only to be shot down – so when people do it, show them appreciation for having tried something.

'At times our own light goes out and is rekindled by a spark from another person. Each of us has cause to think with deep gratitude of those who have lighted the flame within us.'
Albert Schweitzer

TIP: Try these techniques for showing appreciation to others:

Notice when someone does you a favour by:

1) Saying 'thank you' and saying it in public whenever possible.

2) Remembering people's names and using them.

3) Acknowledging effort made – to please, to be efficient, to meet deadlines.

4) Writing and sending a personal note of thanks.

WAY 24

Do you want to go to the party?

I used to know some people who were basket makers and who lived a quiet reclusive life in the countryside. They were happy in each other's company and with a few cherished friends. They admitted to me once that they wanted to be *asked* to 'go to the party' but they didn't really enjoy *going*. They disliked the trivial, superficial nature of the 'party' setting but they still wanted to be asked.

If you don't want to go to the party, for whatever reason, then say 'no thanks'. If you go because you feel you 'ought' you are adding unnecessary stress to your life. On the other hand if you do want to go, and you feel that you could enjoy yourself, you might meet some interesting people and so on, but you fear that you won't know what to say or how to act, then that is the time to be courageous and go, and see what happens. But it is at such times that you need to apply all the other words of advice that have been offered here.

The first thing is to make an honest choice and be true to yourself about whether or not you want to go to the party. It takes courage to admit you want to be invited but you don't really want to go. Of course the party is just an example; it could be a meeting, a business or work opportunity, meeting new people and so on. In fact there is something of an expectation in the modern world that successful people must be gregarious, seek and enjoy the company of others. This can mean we miss out on the creative value of solitude. Quiet contemplation can be a very important source of innovation, of fresh ideas and of renewed energy for being with others.

Susan Cain's book *Quiet* (2012) explains this very powerfully. Solitude matters, it is important to find it, to allow it and to cultivate it. Not that you shouldn't collaborate or cooperate with others, but you should not feel guilty about seeking to be alone with your thoughts or with your reading material or with a small group of friends. She points out how in educational settings these days students are rarely encouraged to conduct solitary work; they are required to sit in 'pods' around a table and work with others. At work open plan offices have become the norm, and the architectural economies justified in some notion of open collaboration. But there are no spaces for contemplation and no escape from the noise and gaze of others.

Yet, as she evidences, most innovative, creative and productive people have their best ideas when thinking alone.

O solitude, the soul's best friend.
How calm and quiet a delight
It is alone
To read, and meditate, and write,
By none offended nor offending none;
To walk, ride, sit, or sleep at one's own ease,
And pleasing a man's self, none other to displease.
Charles Cotton

Try this

It is perhaps one of the hardest practical things to do in the modern world – finding a quiet place of contemplation and solitude. There are always so many people, so much traffic, other people's noise and so on. But if you look you can either find such a place or you can create the 'space' yourself. Look inside and decide where and when you feel most on your own but safe and 'protected' – where do you feel most comfortable with yourself?

Think about where you like to go with other people. Why not go just with yourself? Outside you could try an art gallery, museum, bookshop, department store, aquarium, a public park or public garden.

At home you could take a bath, or choose the quietest room in your own house – turn off phones, Internet, and doorbell!

This is the time an MP3 player comes into its own – your own carefully chosen music, earphones in and you might not get interrupted. (You may even choose to leave the earphones in without the music. In that way people are less likely to interrupt you and you can think without the interruption of other sounds.)

If you have a garden make it as private as you can – with fences, walls or hedges. That way you can control any 'disturbances' from neighbours. Spend time just sitting or strolling there – it is not always a place of 'work'.

Some people take their dog for a walk just to find such quiet time. I have a friend who loves walking around a city. He loves the anonymity of the urban environment – he walks for hours just watching people, and nobody acknowledges him since that is how people behave in a city.

I can't know what suits you. You need to discover this place for yourself. You might even try the 'favourite place' relaxation mentioned below in Way 26.

1 2 3 4 5 6 7 8
9 10 11 12 13 14
15 16 17 18 19
20 21 22 23 24
25 26 27 28 29
30 31 32 33 34
35 36 37 38 39
40 41 42 43 44
45 46 47 48 49

Chapter 8

'INTERIOR' DESIGN: THE ART OF REARRANGING YOUR MENTAL FURNITURE

'When all within
is peace,
How nature
seems to smile.'

William Cowper

WAY 25 Mental toxins

A lot of the activities we engage in can be likened to a game: our work, our leisure time and even relationships with family and friends. Tim Gallwey points out (1975) that all games have an 'inner' and an 'outer' part to them. The outer game is the one we are conscious of all the time – the one with the rules and techniques that we study hard to master. We play it in the outside arenas of the home, the office, the court or the golf course. The inner game, on the other hand, is played in the arena of our mind and all too often we are not aware of it. Clearly the games are interconnected and success depends on how we play both games. However, the inner game is the one we often forget to focus on and take care of. While we attend to the outer game and follow the rules and techniques, it is the inner game that can undermine all our efforts if we do not take care of it.

Our inner life contains a mix of doubts, hopes, fears, anxieties and expectations that can confuse and distract us from playing any game to the best of our ability. This mix of emotions, beliefs and attitudes can create a mental 'toxicity' that undermines and interferes with our natural 'performance' ability.

Think about going for an interview for a job. I have found my most successful interviews happened when I didn't let my strong desire to get the job get in the way of performing well in the interview. In fact I often did best when I didn't really care about getting the job! The trick, of course, is to find those aspects of your inner game that can work for you, and put to one side those which interfere with and obstruct your performance.

During my clinical practice I was approached by an amateur golfer who was gaining great success, but often 'fell at the last hurdle', in the final of any competition. He had friends who were professionals but he had another full-time job and played in competitions during his leisure time. However, his true love was golf and he wanted to turn professional but was frustrated by always losing in the final stages. His strong desire to win, as a solution to achieving his aspirations, was getting in the way of his natural ability at golf. During the rest of the competition he was relaxed because he hadn't arrived at the 'crunch' point when, if successful, he could start to steer towards his career goal. After examining all his interactions at this point in the game it became obvious that his fear of failure was growing and was not helped by his professional friends constantly reassuring him that he *could* 'do it'. We needed to distract him from those anxieties to allow his natural ability to be sustained right through to the end of the competition. So we devised a series of rituals that focused his mind on more trivial things in the approach to the final round: things like which clothes he would wear and how, putting his golf shoes on away from the changing rooms, even tying his laces in a special way, and not talking to anyone. He practised this away from formal contests and, I am delighted to say, when he applied it in formal competition he won his next three tournaments.

Gallwey calls these obstacles 'self-interference'. To get rid of these toxins you need first to examine what they are and how they affect you.

WORST

Think about your worst ever moment. What exactly was bad about it?

How did you feel?

What were you thinking at the time?

(You might consider writing these thoughts and feelings down.)

BEST

Now do the same for your 'best ever' moment. What exactly was good about it?

How did you feel?

What were you thinking at the time?

(Again write these thoughts and feelings down.)

MAKE LISTS:

WORST...

For the **worst** moment – list your thoughts. They might be things like...

- fear of losing control
- doubts about ability
- worry about others (how they might act or think)
- anxiety about being judged
- forgetting things
- being blamed.

Do the same for your physical feelings:

- shaking
- tension
- dry mouth
- breathlessness
- perspiring
- nausea.

Now make two lists for your **best** moment:

Thoughts might be:

- enjoyment
- satisfaction
- happiness
- achievement.

And feelings might be:

- calm
- relaxed
- breathing
- stability.

Try this

What this exercise is designed to do is to enhance your conscious awareness of how you are playing your inner game. If you find that you need to get rid of some toxic thoughts, what follows are some ideas to encourage you to allow the positive ones to come through. I recognise that you cannot do this by merely denying the toxins: you must allow yourself to be fully aware of them when they occur.

TIP: If you are breathless – notice it. **If you are tense – be** fully aware **of it.**

If you have doubts about your ability – acknowledge **the doubts.**

Once you attend to these feelings and thoughts you can also notice that they do not stay the same. They go up and down. If they can go up, they can go down again. If they can go down they can stay down. If other thoughts and feelings from your best moments have been experienced, you can allow them to appear. And you can allow them to rise and dominate.

One easy way to do this is to pick one task at a time and allow yourself to be good at it. It does not matter what it is. It might be painting and decorating a room. It might be playing a game of table tennis. It might even be reading a book comfortably and thoroughly.

I used to do this when playing squash. I would ask a friend to play some practice sessions. We did not have to compete in a game and try to beat each other, merely to run through practice routines for 30 minutes. It could be just as energetic as, but even more fun than, winning and/or losing. I now do it with music. I play guitar or piano in a completely improvised manner (no favourite tunes) for a period of time. With the music, the squash or decorating a room I would take the greatest pleasure in merely doing the task and doing so in full awareness.

And do remember the other sources of mental toxins we referred to earlier: television, radio, popular music, tabloid newspapers and so on. This holds true for smartphones, tablets and gaming devices. Sometimes the undermining thoughts occur because we compared ourselves with someone on television, someone who seems funnier, more in control, better looking.

Control those sources of toxicity too. Remind yourself just how artificial the production of those images is. Remember those people are just as human as you in 'real life' and they play the game of constructing media images because that is their profession. Underneath, most people are struggling with the same uncertainties and anxieties as the rest of us.

I once attended a highly intellectual seminar in which a scholar was giving a lengthy and profound talk that I struggled to understand. Across the room I noticed a young woman taking notes, nodding occasionally at the speaker and looking very wise. I felt quite small. But on the way out of the room I caught sight of her 'notes' – she had been writing a letter to a friend. I also overheard her comment to another person on the way out: 'What on earth was all that about?' We can be fooled by and fool ourselves by such constructed images.

WAY 26 A favourite place

I regularly teach people to 'visit their favourite place' in their imagination. It is a place of safety, of rest and revitalisation. It can be a real place which they had visited in the past and which they felt had some special qualities for them, or a place entirely of their imagination. People tell me about their favourite places and it is interesting that nobody's special place is ever a chain store coffee bar with the muzak playing, or a supermarket, or shopping mall – and yet that is where people spend so much time. Indeed they often repetitively visit such places in search of retail therapy. But they may not be a source of relaxation. And our minds do occasionally need such a retreat.

If you have the time and the means for getting there then, by all means, visit your favourite place in reality. When I was quite young my favourite place was a riverside where I could watch ferries and liners coming and going. I could get there on a bus without it costing too much and I could walk and sit on the landing stage for hours. In my first teaching post I was fortunate to work in a college placed in a former stately home. During my lunch hour I could walk in solitude in a beautifully laid out Italian garden. It restored me mentally and physically to face the afternoon's work.

If you can't visit your favourite places in reality, then there is a way of achieving such peace using a mental exercise. Hypnotherapists often teach their clients some self-hypnosis techniques, and the easiest one to learn is called 'progressive relaxation':

Either have a good friend read out the following script to you, or put it on an audio recorder yourself. Make sure it is read out slowly with pauses after each sentence. After you have done it once or twice you will be able to remember it and you will no longer need to hear it read out to you.

Find a comfortable place to sit or lie down where you will not be disturbed for about 30 minutes. Slowly close your eyes and then listen to and follow these suggestions:

'Begin by noticing your breathing. Don't alter it … just notice it for a minute or so. Then take a deep breath in through your nose and breathe it out slowly through your mouth. Do that again once or twice, then return to simply noticing your breathing – being aware of it.

Now imagine a 'wave' of relaxation slowly flowing over, down and through your body from your head to toe. Allow this to happen gently and slowly and as the imaginary wave flows over you, see, in your mind's eye, each set of muscles in your body in turn just relaxing – letting go and releasing. Start with your eye muscles, then your face muscles, then your neck, shoulders and so on all the way down to the tips of your toes. Do this slowly so that you have time to imagine each of those muscles releasing and relaxing in turn, letting go of any tension in your mind and body.

Next visualise yourself standing on a balcony or terrace somewhere really pleasant and beautiful. As you do so you notice a set of steps leading gently off from the terrace and down to somewhere else. You might wonder where that is. Imagine yourself very slowly and safely moving down the steps, one at a time, counting them in your head – 10 pause… 9 pause… 8 and so on all the way down to 1 and, at 1, you step off to find yourself in your very own wonderful, favourite place. It is a place of peace and calm. A tranquil place where you can ease your mind for a while. It might be a real favourite place you have been to before. Or it might be somewhere more wonderful and conjured up entirely out of your imagination.

You can spend time in this favourite place, moving around, or sitting, lying down, resting. You can notice the colours, the sounds, the beautiful aromas of the place. There may be people there or not, there may be flowers and trees or not. It is your place of calm and peace where your body and mind is restored.

You can spend as much time there as you need and then allow yourself to come back to full conscious awareness, gently and slowly.'

Try this

I have often been surprised at the imaginary places people conjure up when doing this. Sometimes it produces a very emotional response, at other times there is just some calm reflection going on. I have found myself on a beach, in a garden or even just in a world of beautiful colours all around me. Do not be surprised whatever comes – allow it and experience it.

You can find other similar rewarding mental exercises you might like to try in *49 Ways to Think Yourself Well* by Jan Alcoe and Emily Gajewski (2013).

WAY 27 Mind changing

We often criticise people for 'changing their mind'. We seem to think it is a flaw and evidence of people not being determined enough, sure enough, or committed enough to see things through. But if things are not going right, then the best thing you can do is to change your mind. By changing your mind you change your body, your goals and, therefore, your path. If things are not going right then to change your mind and change your direction is the most sensible thing to do. In fact, it sometimes requires courage because we often feel safe with the old mindsets (even if they don't work) and it is then easier to blame everyone and everything other than ourselves. It takes courage and an ability to allow things to be different in order to change your mind.

Indeed, most problems are caused by a combination of the way the world is and our attitude to it – our perspective on it. To solve the problem we have to make choices. We could change the world (which may be difficult to do). Or we could change our attitude to it; re-framing in that way is a constructive way to change our minds. Or we could leave things as they are (and put up with it).

If you choose to make no changes and just 'live with it' then be sure that this is a choice you actively make. By not choosing to do either of the first two, you are choosing to do the last by default. Throughout I have stressed the importance of making choices. Since you are designing your life, choosing between options is inevitable. That puts you in control. So even choosing not to choose (that is, leaving things as they are or letting 'fate take a hand') is also a choice.

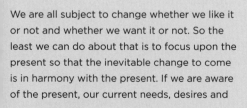

Try this

Listen to yourself.

Trust yourself.

Pay attention to what *you* wish to do to accomplish a goal.

Know that you *can* solve the problem.

We are all subject to change whether we like it or not and whether we want it or not. So the least we can do about that is to focus upon the present so that the inevitable change to come is in harmony with the present. If we are aware of the present, our current needs, desires and plans, then change is more likely to match our intentions.

Ironically, we do tend to have fixed views about change, as I suggested back in Way 3. It is not uncommon for friends and family to say things like: 'You never used to do that' or 'You don't like those foods, clothes, people.' (And they say that while ignoring the possibility that your tastes might have changed.) Or even they challenge you with: 'That's not what you said two (three, four, five etc.) years ago!'

I find that the best reply is: 'That was then, this is now. I thought those things then for various reasons; in fact, thinking those things then has helped me to think what I think now. So this is what I think, feel, know, and need .... now. And you have to know that I might, indeed I probably will, change my mind again in the future.'

At the same time as we resist the idea that our minds are so fickle that we cannot admit to their changing, we are also often engaged in trying to change other people's minds. We might do this as part of our job: in advertising, politics, education or marketing for example. Or merely as part of our normal interactions with people close to us. We might need to change someone's mind about whether they wish to go to the cinema with us instead of staying in and watching TV. The classical study of rhetoric was concerned with the persuasive powers of language. We use rhetoric subtly and often unconsciously when trying to persuade someone to change their views.

Howard Gardner (2004), a professor of cognition and education, suggests that there are seven factors that influence mind changing:

- *Reason*: if a case or convincing argument can be made for seeing things differently.
- *Research*: the existence of evidence backing up the change; some facts.
- *Real world*: a practical readiness for the consequences of change in the world.
- *Resonance*: that the proposed changes 'feel' right.
- *Re-description*: the use of positive expressions instead of negative ones alter how one views the world.
- *Rewards*: it really helps to convince if there are benefits to changing one's mind.
- *Resistance*: it also helps if there exist no excessive obstacles impeding change.

So in preparation for changing a mind, including your own, look at how each of these 'levers' might be operating to help or to hinder the change.

> **TIP:** Don't give up on the idea that you can change other people's ideas, systems and organisations. You can use these levers mentioned above, and remember the words of the Dalai Lama: ' If you think you are too small to make a difference, try sleeping with a mosquito in the room!'

Throughout this book I have been using rhetoric to persuade you not only that change is possible, but, in addition, how you can do it and why it is worth it. I have tried to pay attention to these seven 'R's' of change in order to do that. Indeed you might see any therapeutic encounter as a joint exercise in mind changing. Together we are endeavouring to change how you design your life.

The present UK government even set up a 'Behavioural Insight' team of economists and psychologists who apply these principles to public policy and services. It is commonly known as the 'Nudge Unit', drawing upon the work of Thaler and Sunstein (2009). In essence this approach attempts to get people to make choices that will move them in directions that will make their lives better. It takes account of the factors influencing people's choices and gently 'nudges' them in the right direction by simple arrangements. For instance, I suggested earlier the importance of drinking water. To 'nudge' you into remembering to do this I would suggest leaving a glass of water always ready and filled in a convenient place which would be hard for you to ignore. Each time you pass it you notice it and so will keep up your water intake. (I used to take a filled pitcher of water every morning to my desk. That way it was in front of me and hard to ignore throughout the day. I 'nudged' myself into drinking enough water.)

WAY 28 Source your comfort

When I was young I hated Sunday school. It was enough to be at my ordinary school all week, but then to have to sit in cold church halls playing games with only one theme felt like imprisonment. I struck a deal with my mother that, if I agreed to read the Bible for an hour each Sunday, she would reprieve me from Sunday school. So I did, and the Bible became a source of comfort. Firstly, because it helped me avoid Sunday school of course; but then I started to enjoy the mysteries of its archaic language. Later that language lost its allure for me, but for some people it continues to be a source of comfort throughout their lives. The same is true of most foundational texts: the Koran, the I Ching and so on.

But for those of us who lose the 'connection' to such texts what we need to do is to discover new sources of comfort throughout our lives. One time when I was in great physical pain I came across Arielle Ford's books, beginning with *Hot Chocolate for the Mystical Soul* (1998). I found the short, real accounts of people's remarkable stories heartwarming and uplifting, temporarily distracting me from the pain. In similar vein I have suggested that patients should read Jack Canfield and Mark Vistor Hansen's *Chicken Soup for the Soul* (1993) series. It can be quite uplifting reading about the adversities faced by others and how they survived them, or were helped to survive. Some people find poetry uplifting but, as with all sources of comfort, it must be carefully chosen: I would not advise anyone who is suicidal to read the poetry of Sylvia Plath.

Of course, it need not be a book that provides that comfort. Certain people, places and activities can do it. For example, there is nothing quite like the wise counsel of a true friend.

'No receipt openeth the heart but a true friend, to whom you may impart griefs, joys, hopes, suspicions, counsels and whatsoever lieth upon the heart to oppress it. This communicating of a man's self to his friend works two contrary effects, for it redoubleth joys and cutteth grief in halves. For there is no man that imparteth his joys to his friend but he joyeth the more, and no man that imparteth his griefs to his friend but he grieveth the less.'
Sir Francis Bacon

I've already explained how playing tennis or squash were sources of comfort for me. But for you it could be tenpin bowling, ice skating, playing pool or chess, or watching a film. Quite honestly even an hour with your chosen soap series on TV or radio can be a rewarding form of comfort. And don't forget to use your favourite place as a source of comfort as I suggested in Way 26 or those places of 'quiet' I suggested in Way 24.

Always be prepared to examine the nature of the comfort gained. Notice how it makes you feel. It may only 'work' at that time when you really need it, and you can then move on. From time to time other, new sources of comfort may 'work' for you. Be open to them. Try things out and remain alert to the possibilities.

WAY 29 Using fantasy

It is important to bear in mind what kind of 'creature' we are. Humans are very imaginative beings. Imagination is a faculty and a resource that can be used to help us manage our lives. All too often 'fantasy' is dismissed in a materialist world as being 'unreal'. Yet we fantasise on a daily basis. This might be in the form of daydreams, or when we imagine ourselves as rock superstars when we play our air guitars, or when we are so involved in a film or drama on television that we empathise fully with some characters and detest others.

There are times when fantasy helps us through difficult moments. When being interviewed for a job, or buying a new house we try to 'see' ourselves living in the house or doing the job and what it will mean for our way of life. We imagine whether we will be happy, contented or feel a sense of achievement.

One of the commonest forms of fantasy is the erotic – and perhaps necessarily so. I had a friend who would say of the sex act: 'It's never "natural" is it?' What she meant was that it does seem a strange way to behave for civilised intelligent beings. Indeed, it is an act where we seem to have most in common with animals; it is part of our 'animalistic' nature. But part of the pleasure of sex is the fantasy; whether it be romance or lust. Just think of the nature of 'foreplay'. The play element can be highly imaginative and very variable between people. (See *49 Ways to Sexual Well-being* (2015) by Fran Carter.)

And there are other times of stress and danger when fantasy can help. I once took part in a group therapy exercise in which everyone was to write down their innermost secret on a piece of paper. All the pieces of paper (with nothing identifying who wrote them) were placed in a bundle in the centre of the room. One by one we each took a piece, read out what was on the paper and then were supposed to pretend that the secret was our own and we were telling people about it for the first time. Obviously one had to use a great deal of fantasy to imagine oneself into someone else's deepest, darkest secret. And, of course, subject to random chance, at least one member of the group might have been actually talking about their own secret to a group of strangers. In my group this exercise of telling an innermost secret revealed someone who had always wanted to murder their brother. I'm hoping that they never did it but that 'fantasising' about it might have prevented the actual doing of the act. Indeed, it is possible that the cathartic experience of disclosing the feeling might have dissipated it. Some of the secrets seemed so harmless and benign, one wondered why it would trouble anyone enough to keep them to themselves. But again that is the point – what is really traumatic to one person might be nothing to be concerned about to another. In fantasising and in hearing another fantasise your problem the disclosure without consequence can bring about tremendous release. (I advise always doing this exercise with a group of strangers; not with friends or relatives who might be able to guess your secret!)

At other times fantasy helps us anticipate difficult times – the imagined loss of a loved one helps us both to know that we 'cannot live without them' but also, by imagining their loss, how we would in fact manage to live without them.

Try this

There are many ways to experiment with fantasy. One of the simplest is to find a picture, photograph or painting that you find stimulating and imagine yourself in it. I used to do this with the classical paintings of Alma-Tadema. They exude a kind of perfection not found in ordinary life. Beautiful people reclining on marble benches in perfect weather – not a weed in sight or a hair out of place! Of course it is 'unreal' and that is the point. Advertisers are trying to get you to do this with their product in mind – resist that temptation and imagine your own product or service. For a while you can move around in that imagined world and have a sense of what the 'ideal' could be like.

Learn how to use fantasy well for your own benefit. You might not like the word 'fantasy', but all I want you to think about are 'ideas'. We have 'ideas' about who we are and how we relate to others. Those ideas are the vehicles for our imagination and they guide our actions and our relationships.

'...fantasies fuel our behaviour, revealing our secret hopes and fears and helping us transform our lives... they let us test possibilities. They serve as viable life plans... They create an ambience of hope for the future, even in seemingly hopeless situations, and give us the strength to endure.'
Ethel S. Person

WAY 30 Letting go

A key to rearranging your mental furniture is learning to let go of things that hold you back. Letting go requires you to let life be just as it is in some respects, not challenging it. It requires a great deal of trust: trusting that things will work out right if you set the correct processes in motion. The ability to let go of things is crucial to effecting change in your life. It is not easy but it is essential.

I cannot know what you need to let go of, but I can help you decide. The problem is that we cling to things we once found very useful but which are no longer needed; let them go. There are things you have never used but kept since they seemed potentially useful. Make a judgement: might you use them soon? If probably never – let them go. Of course, you might wish to hold on to 'mementos' that you never use as such – objects, pictures or letters that help 're-mind' you of someone or a place of happiness. If you do, ensure these are mementos that support, inspire and give joy. Make sure they are not obstacles to your progress, things holding you back.

People struggle to let go of books. We keep them after reading but never look at them again. When you have finished with a book, let it go. Clothes are either worn a lot or not at all. But they sit in the wardrobe and we are disinclined to put them on again. If for whatever reason they are no longer fit for purpose, let them go. (I say more about letting go of books and clothes in Way 37.) It is even harder to let go of 'failed' projects; like the half-knitted sweater. No need to finish it: let it go.

Watch out for the 'collecting' disease. Unless it is done with thought and focus, collecting can become a damaging habit. The thoughtless keeping of unnecessary things is a form of informal collecting. The real danger is that collecting becomes an obsession; one which is care-less. Either way these 'not needed' things can get in the way of your progress. If you do not need them, let them go.

You can do this with music you no longer listen to, pens you no longer use, photographs you don't look at and, even, friends you no longer see. It seems callous to let go of friends but, just like objects, they can be 'of their time' and there is a danger of collecting friends as if they were objects. You might have gained a lot from being with them, learning from them, sharing joys and activities. But what you have gained is not lost since it contributed to where you are now. This is not to say 'abandon your friends'; rather it is to say do not feel guilty about those you lose touch with if you have both 'moved on'. A friend who came to our house one Christmas was astonished to see how many cards we had received from friends; she would be even more astonished to see how few cards we now receive. Both we and they decided to no longer only keep in touch at Christmas – we have let them go.

The resistance to letting go comes from the idea that the thing, the object, the person contained something: a plan, a wish, a hope or just a memory.

Just because we have something does not mean we have to use it. There used to be a culinary vogue for 'collecting' a whole range of herbs and spices. They were sold in similar jars and even with a dedicated shelf system for placing in the kitchen. Of course you weren't supposed to use them all each time you made a meal; it would ruin the taste if you did. You follow a recipe and use only those ingredients appropriate to the dish you wish to produce, and you are unlikely to use some of those spices, ever! They were bought because they were part of a 'collection'. They are probably past their sell-by date now; let them go and avoid the temptation of collecting things you are never likely to find a use for.

Wanting and enabling change is part of the objective we are seeking together. Change is going to happen whether we like it or not. Since it will come anyway, 'invest' in it. Acting on these suggestions will give a wonderful sense of freedom.

Recall the biblical story of Lot's wife who was warned not to look back. If you go back far enough all 'we' are is 'salt'; a combination of chemicals. There is a valuable lesson in such metaphors.

So resist looking at the past. 'Re-membering' is putting things from the past 'together again'; it can hurt and, more importantly, it is an unnecessary distraction. You can call to mind what you have learned and apply it to your present and your future. But if you are constantly looking at the past you are facing the wrong way. If you are facing the right direction, all you have to do is keep walking. The trick is to be facing the right way.

It can help to examine our resistance to letting go. Try to answer the following questions:

1) Examine the things you hold on to: pain, pride, jealousy, resentment, or frustration. What do they 'feel' like physically? Close your eyes and ask yourself in what part of your body is your (say) anger? Describe its physical effects on you. What would it feel like not to have those feelings?

2) Do you need to try to control everything in your life? When you can't accomplish such control, how and where in your body do you feel it? What would it feel like to simply let go of the desire to control the natural chaos of life? Examine the events, situations, and people that you feel you need to control. What would it feel like not to hold on to the necessity of doing that?

3) If you have a spontaneous, natural aversion to something, examine your reaction. Precisely what is it you are feeling? Then try to understand why you react in that way. Analyse its components: what is it about that thing that repulses you? What does that say about who you are?

4) Try letting go of everything. Say to yourself: 'Nothing matters; nothing at all.' Don't bind yourself to a specific past. Don't attach yourself to your emotions, people, places or events in the past.

'I have little use for the past and rarely think about it.'
Eckhart Tolle

WAY 31
No 'shoulds'

Obligations bear heavily on our shoulders. If we constantly feel there are things we 'ought' or 'have' to do, we can be weighed down with the concern over what we should do rather than think clearly and assess what is the right or best thing to do. Virgina Satir points out how using these words indicates that people are '…in a dilemma in which they have more than one direction to go at a time.' We wish to do 'x' but we feel we 'should' do 'y'. The contradiction that that creates leaves us with a mental struggle that can put our body into stress and leave us unable to act effectively.

There is another interesting dilemma here though: we are in danger of not watching out for the 'shouldn'ts' too. They can be even more dangerous. 'I shouldn't have that extra piece of chocolate, even though I really would like it.'

The solution is to keep the 'oughts' and 'shoulds' separate from our wishes and desires. So, for example, decide if the 'should' is something that is necessary while the 'wish' can be deferred. Assess which is the most vital at any one time. What you are attempting to avoid is either unthinkingly obeying a social pressure or unthinkingly following a physical desire. The best response is to take time to think what is best for you. Do not react immediately.

Ensure that you see the difference between 'needs' and 'wants'. A need is something you require in order to live: food, air, warmth and shelter. A want is something you feel you lack but wish you had. There are times when our wants can be fulfilled but they should never take precedence over our needs.

'The more you know the less you need.'
Old aboriginal saying

1 2 3 4 5 6 7 8
9 10 11 12 13 14
15 16 17 18 19
20 21 22 23 24
25 26 27 28 29
30 31 **32 33 34**
35 36 37 38 39
40 41 42 43 44
45 46 47 48 49

Chapter 9

'EXTERIOR' DESIGN: THE ART OF REARRANGING YOUR PHYSICAL FURNITURE

'...we are, for better or worse, different people in different places
...it is architecture's task to render vivid to us who we might ideally be.
...We need our rooms to align us to desirable versions of ourselves
and to keep alive the important, evanescent sides of us.'

Alain de Boton

WAY 32 The building

There is only so much work you can do on 'interior' design. You can get your mind to ignore your environment up to a point, but there will come a time when it gets in the way of your progress. So you need a plan for dealing with it.

Most people have heard of *feng shui*, the Chinese art and metaphysics of placement. It is based on the idea that hidden energy (Qi) needs to be allowed to flow correctly to ensure our well-being. In particular this was used to arrange the built environment 'auspiciously', and there are many lessons to be learned about arranging your immediate environment for your physical and mental comfort.

The planning and design of your external life can be just as vital as how you design your inner life. Notice how you feel just right in some environments and yet distinctly uncomfortable in others. With awareness you might realise that the colour of the décor, the kinds of furniture, the height of ceiling and so on are all having subtle effects on how you feel. There is an excellent illustration of this in the work of the anthropologist Carlos Castaneda (1970) who, when under the influence of a hallucinogenic drug, claimed to observe a dog find its 'blue spot'. The dog wandered uncomfortably around until he found an area in front of the house that seemed just right for him to curl up and settle down. Castaneda could 'see' the blue aura exactly where the dog seemed most comfortable. We too need to find our blue spot.

As to choosing the right building, evidently the money you have at your disposal will be vital, but even with constraints such as material resources you still need to bear in mind what is best for your comfort. A country cottage may suit some people very well; the tranquillity offered by a rural retreat with time for contemplation has an appeal. On the other hand you may be the sort of person that needs people around you, to hear and see the hustle and bustle of the city, and who prefers a loft space in a city centre. Keep in mind your needs and preferences and choose the location that suits your needs at the time. And you *are* allowed to change your mind later as your needs change. So if you are lucky enough to be a property owner, do think in terms of how 'saleable' a property might be before you buy so that you retain the freedom to change your mind.

After being brought up in a suburb of a large city I needed a quieter village experience. After I while I missed the city and chose an apartment in the centre of a medium sized town. After enjoying that for a time I chose a small village experience, and that was followed by a seaside apartment. After years again in a city centre with no garden I now live in a house in a small village with a large garden. I have found advantages and disadvantages to all these locations. Apartments always have problems of other people's noise and restrictions on privacy – as do most city centre locations. Rural life can be too remote from amenities and can be demanding in terms of neighbours intruding upon your privacy, while that can be counterbalanced by their friendship and support in times of crisis.

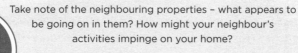

When choosing a place to live visit it several times,
on different days of the week and at different times of the day.

If visiting it in the summer imagine what it will be like
in the winter – and *vice versa*.

Take note of the neighbouring properties – what appears to
be going on in them? How might your neighbour's
activities impinge on your home?

Walk around the property several times, stand and
notice the 'roomscapes', look out of the windows.

Imagine how the property will look with your belongings in it.

Obviously, there may be times when your choices are restricted. You might only have the resources to rent your accommodation. Even so the lesson is to be clear about the implications of your residential location, think through what your life might be like there and the possibilities for change – either within the building or by moving elsewhere. There are 'blue spots' for humans as well as for dogs. Be prepared to seek them out. And if a situation is not ideal you need to find a way to enhance its blueness.

WAY 33

The room

There are many ways to create your blue spot within a building if you give thought to how you arrange your rooms.

> **'The true secret of happiness lies in taking a genuine interest in all the details of daily life.'**
> *William Morris*

Never try to organise a whole room in one go. Do it in a step-by-step manner, otherwise you will get really frustrated. Take one drawer, or one bookcase or one set of files per day. You will feel that you achieved something and you won't be too daunted by the task ahead.

Have a place for everything and put things back in their place when you have used them. Think about the ergonomics of use: where should the cups and saucers be ready for use? Where best to keep glasses? At home we have wall racks for plates so we choose plates that look good on a wall, but they are also easily available to use and not stacked hidden in a cupboard somewhere.

Paint colour is very important. We once inherited a room painted a deep dark red and I wondered why I was often so angry! The trick is not to think of fashionable colours, instead take care to discover how colours make you feel. Often it is best to choose mild, neutral colours for the walls and ceiling. If you wish for some colour variety, you can provide it with your choice of hanging pictures or clocks. After all, those items are fairly easy to remove and/or change.

Think about where you place the sofa. It governs the dynamics of interaction in the room. Do all chairs face the television? Or the fireplace? Or each other? If you have many rooms you can change them according to what you wish to do in the room. If you only have one room you must think more carefully about the dynamics. We used to have all the chairs looking at each other and the TV hidden in a cupboard. People used to come into the room and say immediately: 'I see you don't have a TV.' (Interesting that that was the first thing they noticed.) In fact it was because we wished to only orient the seating to the TV when we had the specific intention to watch it. The rest of the time we wanted to encourage looking at each other and talking and reading. So the position and nature of seating and lighting became more important.

And, as with every other piece of advice I have offered you here, you can change your mind. Arrange the room with your main needs in mind, and if it doesn't work you are allowed to change it.

The same principles apply to your office space if you are lucky enough to have one. Personally I hate open plan offices, since I used to need to have personal telephone conversations or interviews and they were always inhibited if others could overhear. Others enjoy the bustle of such an open office. Whatever the constraints it is important to think of two main things: how to get as much daylight on your desk as possible, and ensure that what you are looking at is to your choice.

There is something atavistic about our need to
be aware of our 'defensible space'.

At a very fundamental, animalistic level we need to be aware of
who or what is around us and how they may approach us. Ethologists
call this the 'umwelt' – the world immediately around us. So:

Organise rooms in terms of sight lines. Ensure you can see 'comings and goings'
from all seating points in a room.

Never place a chair so that you have your back to a door.

If you have to do that, make sure
the door is closed when you are seated.

Ensure doors can be opened
and closed fully when necessary.

Have a desk or reading chair with natural light from a window
to light it and so that you can look out.

WAY 34 The chair

Choose chairs carefully. My wife and I once had two high-backed wing chairs chosen for comfortable reading. They were ideal for our needs at the time, but we noticed that we spent less time being physically close to one another. They were no longer 'fit for purpose'. So we sold the chairs and bought a sofa on which we would spend time together, holding hands.

When choosing your seating system, think about your needs, and comfort. Test out chairs fully before purchase. Colour, texture and 'fashionability' are all less important than comfort.

I learned a lesson about chairs years ago when my boss treated himself to an 'executive chair'. It was expensive: all black leather and chrome, rotating and high-backed with a raise/lower lever. The thing was that my boss was only short and the chair much bigger than him. As I entered his room to discuss an issue, all I could see was the back of the executive chair. I called out: 'A, are you here?' At which the chair swivelled round to reveal him sitting with his legs dangling off the chair like a young child. It undermined any attempt at appearing authoritative. (He realised his mistake later, declared the chair to be 'uncomfortable' and gave it to me!)

> **TIP:** Never buy a chair without sitting in it and testing out how well it works for your intended purpose. 'Desk' chairs need to do different things from 'reading' chairs, and both are different from 'TV' chairs. Never buy a chair for either colour or comfort alone – it must fulfil both purposes.

This is not trivial. It is not. Comfort and appearance are essential 'furnishing' items that are part of how we are seen and how we feel. During the Cold War, when talks about strategic arms limitations were taking place, social psychologists regularly conducted studies on seating position and its effects on negotiations and leadership. They found that leaders emerged amongst those who sat facing the most people – not from amongst those who were sitting side by side. It often resulted in talks being conducted at round or oval tables. In that way, everyone was 'facing' everyone else! If where you sit and how you sit can affect diplomacy, it can certainly be a key consideration to decisions in our personal lives.

Whenever I enter a meeting room, whether chairing or participating, I think first about my needs. If I need to stay quiet and observe I choose a seat away from the action. If I expect to be an active participant I elect to sit where most people in the room can see me and I can see them.

'If you want a golden rule that will fit everything, this is it: Have nothing in your house that you do not know to be useful or believe to be beautiful.'
William Morris

WAY 35 The bed

We spend so much of our lives in bed that this, too, is an important item of furniture. Bed is for sleeping and making love, sometimes for reading and resting but nothing else. Keep the bed and the room it is in as simple, clean and as natural as possible. Choose natural textiles for sheets and covers and an organic mattress. The frame of the bed should be of wood, not metal.

The bed and bedroom must serve to enhance our sleep so that we get the best rest possible to restore our mind and body. I think one of the most troubling technological developments I have ever seen is the television that rises out of the footboard at the bottom of the bed. Avoid watching television in bed. Indeed keep any electrical or electromagnetic sources out of the bedroom.

> **TIP:** Make a list of all the factors present when you have a good night's sleep and a list of all those things that seem to bring about a bad night for you. Then set about ensuring you have more of the former than the latter in your bedroom.

Far too little attention is paid in our 24 hour society to the quality of our sleep. But testimony to the importance of sleep can be seen by the existence of international associations, major research centres in distinguished universities across the globe and more than one scholarly journal devoted to its study. If you need to know more have a look at the Stanford Center for Sleep Science and Medicine (http://sleep.stanford.edu/).

In my clinical practice I regularly had patients with sleep problems and invariably they failed to control their sleep environment adequately. One young single man was exhausting himself at work since he had inadequate sleep during the night. He would arrive home late, eat a takeaway pizza in his bedroom while watching television, play an action game on his computer for an hour or so, then light a candle since he believed it would 'calm him down', then close the window and curtains – and fail miserably to get to sleep.

His errors should be obvious: the bedroom had become a place of activity not of rest, the candle took all the oxygen out of the air, which was exacerbated by keeping the window closed. After a few nights of no TV/computer in the bedroom, no food, curtains closed against outside street lighting but window open a little for air, his sleep patterns began to improve.

Chronic sleep deprivation can undermine all your other efforts at improving your well-being.

'Bring us to our resting beds weary and content and undishonoured; and grant us in the end the gift of sleep.'
Robert Louis Stevenson

WAY 36 The garden

It is certainly a privilege to have some outside space in your home environment. I have been fortunate enough to experience a range of different garden opportunities from an acre of land to window boxes. If you have none of your own then take time to enjoy the space in public parks or gardens.

'I grow plants for many reasons: to please my eye or to please my soul, to challenge the elements or to challenge my patience, for novelty or for nostalgia, but mostly for the joy in seeing them grow.'
David Hobson

I have spent hours wandering around National Trust gardens – just watching, breathing and thinking. At home planting, watching things grow, experiencing their presence and beauty and picking vegetables, fruit and herbs for our kitchen brings me much pleasure.

I have two warnings:

Size: Don't have a garden so large and demanding that you are unable to manage it, unable to keep it looking as you would wish and so get frustrated. If you only have access to a small garden, think carefully about what you choose to plant and maintain.

Content: Choose colours, shapes and culinary use with care. A vegetable garden can require constant attention. Some flowers and vines look after themselves. Herbs are always rewarding if only for aroma.

'The glory of gardening: hands in the dirt, head in the sun, heart with nature. To nurture a garden is to feed not just the body, but the soul.'
Alfred Austin

The importance of gardens is easily seen in how they feature in literature, myth and legend: starting with the Garden of Eden as the lost foundation of human peace and contentment. There were also the hanging gardens of Babylon, and who could fail to be captured by the idea behind Frances Hodgson Burnett's story of *The Secret Garden*? Communal gardens and gardening in urban brownfield sites have brought people together in ways that other social measures cannot.

'A garden is a grand teacher. It teaches patience and careful watchfulness; it teaches industry and thrift; above all it teaches entire trust.'
Gertrude Jekyll

WAY 37

One drawer at a time

Therapist David K. Reynolds founded an approach called 'constructive living' which draws mainly on two Japanese therapies: Morita and Naikan. Morita is similar to 'Feel the fear and do it anyway'; it says recognise that you have fears and don't try to deny them since that is to deny reality – we can't be free of our anxieties all the time. In some respects anxiety can be adaptive, having us exercise caution when necessary. Naikan is a more contemplative approach to how we think about other people: for each person we are in a relationship with it asks us to reflect on what was received from some person, what was done in return for that person and what troubles and worries were caused by that person.

Morita uses mundane practical activities to distract us from the anxieties that overwhelm and limit us. Thus as an in-patient treatment, Morita advocates leaving a patient in bed for a week with just their three meals a day and normal physiological functions. They dwell on all their concerns and worries and regrets, but after a while they need a distraction from these concerns and are allowed to, say, sweep the floor of their room for a fixed period of time. The mundane act of sweeping gives them a rest from their thoughts, and as each day progresses they are allowed a little more mundane activity such as more cleaning and tidying. The point is that eventually they sweep the floor because they wish to keep it clean, not merely as a distraction from painful thoughts. In a similar way, choosing to clean and tidy a drawer or a cupboard can firstly distract from concerns, secondly be rewarding in itself (tidy drawer = tidy mind), and then have a functional benefit, making it easier to remember where things are and find them.

There is a crucial lesson, though, about tidying. Do only one drawer at a time. Take pleasure in the success of having tidied that drawer – fully relish the experience. Ensure it is easy to find the things in it; don't overfill. That's enough for today. Get on with other pressing tasks.

Tomorrow is another drawer.

In the same way, cleaning the path or the kitchen or the wardrobe can be rewarding in itself since you are better able to use any facility that is clean, tidy and organised for use. It is part of keeping things simple.

The same principles can be applied to all your belongings. Allow some time every day or every week simply for getting organised – if you don't you can end up spending all your time just organising and not getting anything creative or productive done. The rationale for managing time, place and space is related to empowerment. By managing the environment you manage yourself.

Try this mental experiment:

Imagine you have to move house due to an imminent disaster and you can only take one suitcase. What will you put in it? That's a real test of what you really 'need' in your life. (This exercise can also help in avoiding unnecessary spending. Think twice about anything you buy – do you need it? Do you want it? Would it go in the suitcase?)

Take care with what you 'collect' and apply the principles of 'letting go' I suggested earlier. Although we like books my wife and I have divested ourselves of at least three of our 'libraries' throughout our life together – we have sold or given away most of the books we had at the time. Now, if you are booklovers you might be horrified at that prospect. You might even think we were probably moving house and saw the sense in not taking all the books with you. Well, I wish we had been that sensible. We once had to rent storage space to keep more than 200 boxes of books which we then had to pay to be removed And when we eventually got those books to our new home we realised that we really didn't need most of them and had been holding on to them largely for sentimental reasons, or because they were 'good' books; not because we wanted to read or use them again. So what we asked ourselves was: 'When did we last read or use that book?' And: 'Might I need that again in the near future?' If not it merely becomes a possession to put on show in our library as a reminder to ourselves of a book we once enjoyed, or a form of display to others of acquired knowledge, or because the decoration on the spine matched our room

decoration. All pathetic reasons for hanging on to them! So in the space of a couple of months we sold over 2,000 books. And we still haven't missed them more than three years later. And there's less dust, fewer opportunities for creatures to infest the paper and, most importantly, clarity in our minds that the books that are still in our lives really *do* matter.

You can do the same with clothes. How many items do you have hanging in your wardrobe or in a drawer that you have not worn in a year, or more? It might have once been precious, you wore it regularly or on special occasions and so cannot part with it. It might not even fit now or not suit current fashion. It is there gathering dust, or even worse creatures, it is occupying your mind and your time even just moving it and cleaning. Let it go. Replace it with something that refreshes you as well as your wardrobe. Clothes are not trivial items. They are part of your identity and are important to how you feel about yourself and whether you are comfortable. It is not just vanity; it is a skin extension and vital to how you see yourself, usually through others' reflections of the 'presentation' of your self.

Don't keep any clothes you don't use 'just in case'. This is a part of 'exterior' design that affects your 'interior'. The old things hanging in the wardrobe are occupying your mind too. Only have the items you need and use regularly. If the old things are still in good condition they will not be wasted in the local charity shop; someone else can give them a new life. Put away unseasonal clothes. Only have available in your immediate wardrobe those clothes currently in use. Arrange them so they are easy to find – trousers together, jackets together, matching outfits together. All this removes the need for unnecessary decision-making about what to wear and when.

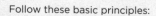

Follow these basic principles:

Throw away, give away or sell whatever you don't use.

Have those things around you which give you pleasure.

Have those things you use near to hand and easy to access.

Sort things first; purge next – getting rid of anything not needed or used; then 'file' for easy future access to those things you are keeping.

Try this

When we were first married my wife decided something similar for my then current collections. Boxes of sweet and chocolate wrappers from delights I had known; a 'magnificent' collection of beer mats from the 1950s and 1960s from more 'mature' delights. I joke now that they would be worth a fortune, but they wouldn't really, and I would have been wasting my time carting them around from house to house and finding storage space for them. I am forever grateful she helped me dispose of them all those years ago; and I have never missed them.

By clearing your wardrobe, and your bookshelves, and your beer mat collection, you are clearing up your physical and mental environment at the same time. If you need more help with clearing up the unnecessary have a look at Marcie Lovett's *The Clutter Book*.

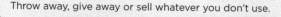

1 2 3 4 5 6 7 8
9 10 11 12 13 14
15 16 17 18 19
20 21 22 23 24
25 26 27 28 29
30 31 32 33 34
35 36 37 **38 39**
40 41 42 43 44
45 46 47 48 49

Chapter 10

MENTAL CONTRACTS

'If you don't deny yourself for others they look upon you as detestably selfish; but they bear with astonishing fortitude the ills you may incur by the sacrifices you have made for their sakes.'

W. Somerset Maugham

© depositphotos.com

WAY 38 Does that work for you?

One of the problems with personal relationships, in families and at work, lies in the undeclared mental contracts that people draw up. Sometimes one party to a relationship draws up a mental contract without consulting the other party, and keeps it to themselves while mentally 'signing up' to their part of the contract. To make matters worse they get upset when the other party doesn't fulfil the obligations to a contract they haven't seen, didn't agree to and don't even know is being applied to the relationship.

It is unfair and impossible for the other party to live up to. You will find yourself disappointed by a friend who doesn't know about your unwritten and unspoken contract. Understanding such mental contracts is a useful way of coming to terms with our personal relationships and managing them to everyone's best advantage. Examine what contracts you have set up for the people in your life and how little they know of that contract. If you need to attend to the relationship then share elements of the contract with them and see if they are willing to live up to it. Moreover, are you willing to accept the terms of the contract? Reflect on what you owe them in return.

To illustrate, notice how many of the problems that occur in family relationships revolve around unspoken 'contractual' details and coping with the inevitable changes in the structure of the family, the roles we play and alterations in our status as we grow and change. We have notions about the ideal family life which we aspire to even when we recognise it to be a fiction. We sometimes create such myths about our own family's history. Watch a young family at the seaside, in the park or at the fair, or when out shopping. The youngest members have only been a part of that group for a few short years. They might have experienced little direct change themselves but this represents 100% of their own life experience and they endow it with an unrealistic sense of permanence.

Coming to terms with difference is the secret of success in handling one's inherited baggage, the unspoken mutual expectation we impose upon each other. The greatest pressure that members of a family apply is the assumption that everyone in the family is (thinks, feels) the same, and/or the assumption that they know you better than anyone else could. Instead of celebrating sameness when the family has to get together they should really celebrate their differences. Go out there and allow yourself to be different with gusto, even when with your family. And allow them to do the same. Don't constrain each other with expectations of sameness and don't be indifferent to them. You can all be as different as you wish!

Of course the same applies to other personal relationships. What expectations do you hold of others without telling them? Some of the best understandings of this process I have found in the work of Dr. Phil McGraw, whose key question about mismanaged relationships is: 'How is that working for you?' He asks blunt, direct and trenchant questions about problematic relationships. All too often when we have a problem we forget to change our responses, and then we wonder why the problem continues.

Take the example of anger. There is an assumption amongst civilised people that we should not get angry. We might be advised to 're-frame'. Yet nothing is more calculated to exacerbate anger than to suggest to an angry person that they ought to re-frame. If you are fortunate enough to generally allow things to wash off you then anger is brief and easily dissipates. But we have to recognise that not everyone is like that. Burying anger is harmful. It tightens our core supporting muscle – the psoas – and can freeze us rigid, causing us further pain and hurting even those we are stopping ourselves from being angry with.

I can give you an example. Cal was having a very difficult time handling the death of her mother. After going through the trauma she wrote to two people she felt were really good friends. She emptied her heart out to them. But she got nothing in return. Not even the briefest of sympathetic responses. When they lost their parents Cal had written to them letters of compassion and support. She got nothing back from them then, but forgave them in their time of grief, and anyway she hadn't written to seek a reply. She had written out of sympathy. But she was disappointed when she lost her own mother in their failing to even acknowledge her need and despair. She tried to re-frame, tried to think

well of them: perhaps they didn't know what to say or how to say it, and then she got angry but couldn't allow it. It caused pain, and illness until she voiced her anger – not to them, though that could have been ideal even if it ended the friendship. It was no longer hurting her. They had 'shown who they were' and that should be enough.

You can see that Cal had established a mental contract without consulting her friends. She had an understanding of what friends are for without sharing that with them. She had imposed contractual obligations on them that they didn't even know about. To cap it all she quelled her anger instead of letting it out.

It might have helped if she had borne in mind therapist Carl Rogers' key insight of holding 'unconditional positive regard'. Sometimes you clarify the contract, other times you recognise what cannot be clarified. So there is no harm in letting go of friends who cannot offer the kind of friendship you need. Russel Harty said: 'A friend is someone who doesn't care what time you get up in the morning'. A wonderful guide for the core of friendship is to understand your friend to the best of your ability and let them know that; but not at the expense of your own mental and physical health.

Try this

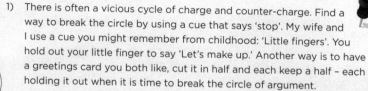

Dr. Phil has a suggestion for couples who find themselves in conflict:

1) There is often a vicious cycle of charge and counter-charge. Find a way to break the circle by using a cue that says 'stop'. My wife and I use a cue you might remember from childhood: 'Little fingers'. You hold out your little finger to say 'Let's make up.' Another way is to have a greetings card you both like, cut it in half and each keep a half – each holding it out when it is time to break the circle of argument.

2) He also advises taking each other by the hand when trying to have a disagreement.

These are better 'contracts' to use for resolving a dispute.

WAY 39 Picking a lane

My wife still says to me: 'Pick a lane', when she sees me wandering about, not just in one field, but in lots of fields. And the highway metaphor is very apt since I have what might politely be called 'eclectic' interests. I am fascinated by so many things. But she is right that there are times when I should be on a route, with a clear destination. It does not have to be just one lane; it can be a three-lane motorway – but not an eight-lane one! That's just too much to handle. It doesn't mean you cannot change lanes; but do so decisively, with good reason. Again this illustrates the need to make a conscious choice: *Choose your lane*.

Knowing where you are going helps to keep you on the right track.

Even when travelling down the highway it can be the assumption of permanence that is our undoing. Once in our lane we are in danger of assuming that things will stay the same. They don't. Change is inevitable. So we may be cruising along and not anticipate a traffic jam or road closures. Coping with it is not enough – being part of it is much more fulfilling. Be prepared to amend your route if unforeseen events require it.

This metaphor is very important for your project. Throughout I have stressed how important it is for you to have a 'destination' in mind – to aim towards a goal. You have to know where you are going. But it is equally vital not only to allow yourself to change lanes from time to time, in other words to have a few destinations in mind, but also to change the highway you are on and accept that the

original destination you had in mind is no longer relevant to you.

This is not necessarily an easy thing to accept. To pursue a goal you have to be a little focused, 'single-minded' or tenacious. And it may be a fear of failure that stops you reconsidering your goals, or a rigid adherence to a 'mental contract' that you made – with yourself! But to pursue a goal that is no longer rewarding to you can undermine your best efforts. While you were travelling down that lane you will have learned a great deal – indeed the recognition that a different destination is required is a vital learning point.

So from time to time I want you to re-visit an exercise I suggested in Way 7:

Conduct an updated personal 'vision workshop'.

Write down what you are doing now.

What is good about it?
What is not so good about it?

Write down where you desire to be and what you desire to be doing...
...next week
...next year
...in ten years' time.

Are these the same goals as you envisaged earlier?

Which of the things you are doing now will help you move towards the things you desire?

Keep doing them.

Which will not help?

As soon as you are able, stop doing them.

Now start to think about what extra things you
need in order to take aim at those new goals or to
revitalise your interest in your original goals.

This will help you decide if you wish to stay in the same lane or change lanes, or alter
your 'destination'. There is no right or wrong about this – these are your choices.

WAY 40 Forgiveness

'Hell is other people.'

Jean-Paul Sartre

Take care when 'judging' others. We can often be too quick to judge. You cannot know everything about them to help you make that really informed judgement. Give them some 'benefit of doubt' when they do something you disapprove of. The more we know about people, the more we can understand why they might engage in behaviour which we do not like. But we rarely know all there is to know about why people do the things they do. To be 'understanding' is not to know everything about other people – rather it is to know that we do not know, and cannot know, everything about them.

That realisation is important in the 'hidden contract' we have with other people. It is the foundation for building an ability to forgive without judging. In fact, as psychiatrist Dr. Gerald Jampolsky (1983) says: 'Forgiveness is just another form of letting go.'

Florence Scovel-Shinn offers another ancient saying: 'No man is your enemy, no man is your friend, every man is your teacher.'

'I have learnt silence from the talkative, toleration from the intolerant, and kindness from the unkind; yet strange, I am ungrateful to these teachers.'

Kahlil Gibran

Arguments and conflict are to some degree inevitable in life. But there are ways of engaging in an argument that can help sustain your authenticity. Take an argument with a loved one. While you are really annoyed with them, even angry about something they said or did, throughout the confrontation remember one thing: that you love them and are loved by them. It can be hard to bring this to mind in the heat of the moment but if you do it makes it easy to 'forgive' them their point of view and to repair any damage caused. In fact, sometimes when you bear this in mind, the heat of the moment can just dissipate, the argument seems pointless in comparison to your love and the argument can be over.

You can even try this with someone who has annoyed you whom you may not actually 'love' – they can be a passer-by who looked disdainfully at you. Begin to forgive them immediately by thinking: nothing was meant by their action or behaviour, and they perhaps didn't even realise that they had offended you. Begin with the thought: 'I have no reason not to like you.' That will make it easier to forgive any thoughtless deed on their part.

Sometimes the even texture of the best of relationships can be 'torn' by an incident or the wrong word. But there is no need to despair about it. The tear needs mending, certainly. Take time, examine how the tear came about and decide to mend it. Sometimes it does take two and the tear can be repaired together. But being able to say 'sorry' is a simple first step in mending a tear.

WAY 41 Nothing is expected

At some point you might decide that it is worth dispensing with the mental contracts – spoken or unspoken – and adopt a new policy that you can give to others and take upon yourself.

TIP: Try telling yourself this: 'Nothing is expected of you.'

Imagine what it feels like if someone were to say that to you. Especially someone who you feel is always expecting things of you – a needy friend or relative. In return give that phrase to someone who you think might think you are needy: nothing is expected of you.

Expectations and obligations imprison us in our relationships. They constrain who we are and who we allow ourselves to be. If we can escape our obligations we can be free in our authentic relationships with others. We can be sure that we will do things because we wish to, not because of expectations imposed on us by others and, worse, by ourselves.

1 2 3 4 5 6 7 8
9 10 11 12 13 14
15 16 17 18 19
20 21 22 23 24
25 26 27 28 29
30 31 32 33 34
35 36 37 38 39
40 41 **42 43 44**
45 46 47 48 49

Chapter 11

CHANCE AND SYNCHRONICITY

© depositphotos.com

'There is an island
of opportunity in
the middle of
every difficulty.'

Anonymous

WAY 42 Seeing an opportunity

Always allow time for serendipity. Watch out for when an angel comes to you and says: 'Have you got 10 minutes? I can tell you something which will change your life.' Don't say: 'Sorry, I'm late for an appointment.'

Do you remember Louis Pasteur's observation about scientific discovery: 'Chance favours the prepared mind'? He was saying that whatever destiny has in store for us will only be effective if we are ready to receive it. Although we must make choices and be in control, we must also accept destiny. William James in *The Will to Believe* celebrated humanity's search for the 'unknown' part of what it is to be human. Both Goethe and Thoreau believed that success is guaranteed by advancing 'confidently in the direction of one's dreams'. They held a view of a Universal Good, cosmic forces or karma that will help or collaborate with us if they are fed something positive. James Redfield's *Celestine Prophecy* depends upon a recognition of synchronicity and opportunity. Deepak Chopra throughout his work advocates a complete detachment from outcomes. Even Coué suggested leaving human 'will' out of it. Autosuggestion works on the basis of the belief that such and such a thing *is* going to happen which amounts to an acceptance of benign destiny. The conscious attempt to 'will' it will only achieve the reverse (Coué 1960: 12–13). The idea is that you position yourself ready for what destiny will bring.

Try this

Say, for example, you want to be a writer.

Imagine you're being interviewed in 10 years from now. You have published several books. Write the interview: tell the world who you are, what you are about, what is your favourite work to date, what motivates you as a writer. The result of this is a blueprint and plan of your writing career.

Do the same – that is imagine the interview – if you plan to be an artist, musician, teacher, gardener, accountant or sports coach or anything else.

While acting, doing, taking responsibility and making choices you must also recognise the need to maintain balance within the natural, cosmic order. But there is no inevitability about such natural constraints. Even apparently fixed biorhythms, with their ups and downs, can be planned for (Crawley 1996).

Instead of asking 'What if...?' and letting a negative perspective on chance and risk obstruct your growth ask 'Now what...?' This leads *you* to take action, to make decisions and to move forward in a positive manner.

'When the wind blows some people build walls, others build windmills.'
Proverb

WAY 43

Not broke? Don't fix it

Most of us have heard the phrase: 'If it ain't broke don't fix it!' and many of us will have tried to act on it. But that can be easier said than done since there are so many temptations to keep trying to 'fix it'. We 'tinker' with things that might be better left alone. Sometimes even when we have found the 'ideal', we struggle to find ways to improve on it.

I can give what you might think is a trivial example of this, but it really is quite important. I narrowed down my chocolate tastes bit by bit (or even 'bite by bite') but gradually came to focus on the chocolate that is just right for me. My taste is simple. It must be organic, dark and preferably above 80% cocoa. Now, you would be surprised at the growing range available even with those narrow criteria; so I keep trying the others and any new ones in the field when, every time, I go back to the few that really satisfy my needs. One of those is Booja-Booja – '...deeply luxurious truffles inebriated with organic fine de champagne' and sounds as good as it tastes. But it also comes with an agreeable philosophy on the box:

> *'It's pleasurable oneness with all that is arising...pure enjoyment...*
> *It's noticing we are not in paradise... and loving anyway...*
> *Relax; nothing is under control.'*

I could say: 'Try them' (and that should secure me at least one box of my favourites). Instead I suggest you find 'yours'... and enjoy whatever your specific tastes require. Discover what you like and stay with it as long as it works. Stay with whatever gives you pleasure and sustains you while keeping yourself open to new discoveries.

WAY 44 Doing the research

The whole point of this book has been to encourage you to take action for yourself – to act on your own behalf. I have tried to inform and inspire you, but only you can maintain the progress you need.

My wife and I have always been careful of our diet and, as a consequence, manage our body weight quite well. A good friend of ours who is, in all honesty, consistently overweight once said: 'I could lose weight if only I lived with you.' That is certainly true but it shows that all too often people will not do for themselves things they believe only others can do for them. I don't think it is mere laziness. It comes from the disbelief that they can act on their own initiative, find out the necessary information for themselves and act on it.

Do the research and continue to look for the information you need to improve your life. I used to say begin with an encyclopedia, these days it might be the Internet and the World Wide Web. So when you finish this book don't stop here! Put the suggestions into action but go on looking for other ideas, suggestions and advice that help you achieve your 'design'. You might begin your own research by looking at the 'Where do I go from here?' notes that I supply towards the end of the book. There is an enormous amount of supportive information out there. Make sure you use it.

A word of caution about further research: you will undoubtedly find a range of contrary opinions and apparently conflicting pieces of evidence for everything you discover. In some respects this too is 'healthy'. Any challenges to facts or debates about evidence keep us thinking about what works. Instead of complaining that the media tell us 'one thing one week and something opposite the next', bear in mind that the evidence we seek is subject to a variety of influences – some more powerful than others. Thus I am always sceptical about the efficacy of a drug when that information is supplied by a pharmaceutical company with a vested interest in the commercial development of that drug. It is just the same when a car salesman waxes lyrical about the car he wants you to buy. He might be inclined to play down any disadvantages. So keep your critical mind alert about any information you receive, and simply try things out for yourself. If they work for you then that has to be good enough.

Let me give you a telling example. Some years ago there were reports in the popular press of some research for the UK Food Standards Agency comparing the 'nutritional content' of organic and conventional foods (fruits and vegetables). It was headline news that the research found 'no difference'. In other words the nutritional content of conventionally produced foods was no worse than that of organic produce. You already know that I have suggested on a few occasions the importance of natural, organic food sources for our health. Then I heard an interview with the lead researcher and he was asked: 'Does this mean that organic food is no healthier than conventionally produced food?' He replied carefully: 'Our research was not about "health", it was to compare nutritional content.' Personally, I was not at all surprised that the research found no difference in nutritional content. And that is not what particularly concerns me – but 'health' does. So I could say the research was asking the wrong question for me. What I really want to know is: which food does least damage to me physically, which is least toxic and which does most good? (I might also be interested in which tastes better!)

So when you do your own searching for evidence take special care to examine what question the research was asking. Test its relevance to your needs. Then look at who is doing the research and who for? What are their motives and intentions? Do they have any obvious prejudices?

'Nothing is more powerful than information, especially when it is abused... Information is a beacon, a cudgel, an olive branch, a deterrent – all depending on who wields it and how.'

Steven D. Levitt and Stephen J. Dubner

© freepik.com

WAY 45

Make room for miracles

The owner of a guest house where we stayed in France e-mailed me to say that someone we knew had been staying there. Meg was an old friend from North Wales and she and her family were spending Christmas at the guest house. We had lost touch and I hadn't seen her for ten years. The guest house owner had learned that she was a hypnotherapist and had mentioned that another regular guest, me, was also a hypnotherapist. Meg asked the name of this other guest and realised it was me. The last time we had met, we had bumped into each other on a professional development course – both of us had decided to study clinical hypnosis quite independently of each other. Again, we had lost touch for the previous ten years. We now both live in France and she lives less than an hour's drive away – in the same town as another friend of ours who used to live in the same part of North Wales as we did, but who had never met Meg. It is as if we made similar choices in our lives without sharing with the others and here we find ourselves in touch again.

You might regard all that as not so much of a 'miracle', more a set of not very remarkable coincidences. If you are a rationalist then you might even think of coincidences as being mere 'statistical probabilities'. The interesting thing is how often some of those 'mere probabilities' can occur and how remarkable they can be. Many distinguished writers, scientists and philosophers have written extensively about such miracles. Carl Jung was fascinated by synchronicity and Rupert Sheldrake has explained coincidences as a form of morphic resonance – as if, on some level and by some means as yet unexplainable, patterns of thought and behaviour are repeated in different times and space. Sheldrake's most popular work (2011) was to do with how pets anticipate the arrival home of their owners by becoming restless in the hour before their arrival and then waiting by the door for them to enter. And they do this even if the owners vary their arrival times deliberately. More recently he has explored the telepathy involved with telephone calls and found that people can often anticipate who will be calling them even without advance warning (Sheldrake 2014).

One thing I have learned about miracles is that you will not see them if you do not expect them. In a similar way simple coincidences can be missed if you are not open to them. Indeed, one way to note and be aware of coincidences is to keep a diary: things might only gain in significance upon later reflection. We forget so many occurrences that it is only if they are recorded that we 'see' their significance.

Some years ago travelling through Middle America my wife and I detoured to the town centre of Louisville, Kentucky. We were looking to find a decent cup of coffee. Having read my 'coffee rules' earlier you realise to us that meant something European: a quality espresso. It proved impossible in the US at that time. American coffee was always fresh but so weak that we ended up drinking too much of it to get anywhere near our regular caffeine supply. As we walked into a shopping mall there came a distinctive aroma – *could it be?* There was a small coffee bar, with genuine espresso machines and a barista. We collected our coffees and had to share a stand-up table with another lady who seemed equally appreciative of quality coffee. Indeed, she travelled a great deal and knew of this coffee bar as the only place to find a good espresso in Middle America. We talked about appreciating taste and quality and I compared this experience to something I remembered from one of my favourite films: *To Sir With Love*. The 'hero' teacher in the film is played by Sidney Poitier and there is one scene in which he recounts his absolute love of the taste of oranges. He played it so well and so powerfully that I can 'taste' the oranges as I think of it now. The woman announced that the film was based on a real person – her husband. And, yes, he did feel exactly that way about oranges.

There may be no fundamental 'message' from coincidences, except that there are things beyond the mundane that remind us of the remarkable nature of human existence. On the other hand I would not want to rule out the possibility that coincidences are meaningful and can help us if we take note of them.

I have written elsewhere about a range of events that occurred after my mother-in-law's death, but one incident serves to make this point. The loss of a loved one always challenges us to reflect on the past, what was missed and what was accomplished in relationships, what the future holds in terms of further loss. But we all seek comfort at such times. My mother-in-law's name was Ann. We parked in a near empty car park to go to the Registrar's office to register her death and when we returned to the car another person had parked right next to us with the registration plate ****ANN.

There are excellent books about coincidences written by Ken Anderson who has compiled a range of similar experiences and attempts to make some sense of them by linking to other literature. I recommend *The Coincidence File*

(1999) as a start, and you can follow up the links he makes if it interests you. If, however, you suspect there is nothing particularly miraculous in such coincidences you might look at one of the many books produced by mathematicians that strive to take the magic out of miracles: one such excellent book is by David J. Hand – *The Improbability Principle* (2014). Even the mathematical principles involved are worth exploring; they too are miraculous!

With more space I could tell you more about my personal experiences with synchronicity – such as how I met my wife again after losing touch and now we have been married for over 45 years. Even how we now come to be living in France as a result of our train breaking down in the Channel Tunnel ten years ago. But those are other stories for another time.

> To me every hour of the light and dark is a miracle...
> To me the sea is a continual miracle,
> The fishes that swim – the rocks – the motion of the waves – the ships with men in them.
> What stranger miracles are there?
> *Walt Whitman*

It has become almost trite to comment that the real miracle in life is that we are even here at all. The chances of the earth and its inhabitants being 'created' by accident are so phenomenally small that our existence is by definition miraculous. With that view in mind, however, I have seen the world in a different light. It is not just poetic that the sky is blue and the sea green – it is literally awesome. I included this group of Ways to encourage you to remain aware. Listen to your inner voice. Look out for helpful messages in dreams, in coincidences and in the chance encounter. Who knows how it may benefit you?

1 2 3 4 5 6 7 8
9 10 11 12 13 14
15 16 17 18 19
20 21 22 23 24
25 26 27 28 29
30 31 32 33 34
35 36 37 38 39
40 41 42 43 44
45 **46 47 48 49**

Chapter 12

SCRIPTING YOUR LIFE

© depositphotos.com

'...imagination sets the goal picture which our
automatic mechanism works on. We act, or fail to act,
not because of will, as is so commonly believed,
but because of imagination.'

Maxwell Maltz

WAY 46 Lifescripting

It can help to think of your life as a story. Narratives are important to human beings since they are accounts that people offer to explain their thoughts, feelings and behaviour. Humans are imaginative creatures and we can understand them better when we discover the sources they draw upon to construct that imagination. Those sources are the stories that they have been told, or have told themselves, about themselves throughout their lives.

Telling stories is one of the ways human beings relate to the world and to each other. Stories hold meaning and have a purpose especially when we tell them in our own words. Narrative is one of the most enduring and pervasive forms of human communication because it mirrors things that are common throughout human experience and across communities. It conveys common perceptions of time, of the causes and consequences of human actions, of responsibility and of intent. Narratives represent sequences of events that are linked by continuity of character, scene or agency. In that sense narratives reveal something about the identities both of the teller and those who are being told about.

By helping anticipate and rationalise social action, narratives help steer it. Throughout this project I have been using stories with just those ends in mind. Narrative is found in most human activities. Think of the narrative contained in songs. They set scenes, tell tales, envisage prospects, and jog the memory of past events, dreams or wishes. The song may have a narrative, or it may merely identify protagonists: characterising them as being of a certain type, dressed in a certain way and capable of certain actions. Music also sets the mood to the narrative of people's lives. This might be background muzak in a store, or the MP3 player that allows people to choose their own ambient sounds instead of having it dictated by someone else.

Narratives encapsulate our concepts and assumptions about how the world works and how people relate to each other. Narratives assume a particular place in human understanding and in the maintenance of a social order. Institutionalised storytelling is particularly common across cultures, and storytelling can achieve a range of purposes. Not all storytellers are trying to teach us something. And not all stories contain a deliberate moral intent. But all stories can have such a consequence, since those hearing the story are always capable of drawing their own lessons, of inferring their own intent (Josselson and Lieblich 1993; Reissmann 1993). This means that all narratives can have an effect, a persuasive consequence, whether intended or not, since those effects can depend as much upon something in the audience as something in the storyteller.

The bigger question is the importance of the narrative within which all other narratives are contained – what philosopher Jean-François Lyotard called the 'grand narrative'. This overarching narrative frames all else, helping other 'sub-narratives' to make sense. The grand narrative may be archetypal, something which influences everybody's lives within a culture.

'Narratives...determine criteria of competence and/or illustrate how they are to be applied. They thus define

'what has the right to be said and done in the culture in question, and since they are themselves a part of that culture, they are legitimated by the simple fact that they do what they do.'
Jean-François Lyotard

For example, in the West we used to talk about living in the 'free world' – that assumes that people in the rest of the world are not free, and it also disguises those aspects of our world that really stop us from being free. After all, we are bound by certain political and economic structures and they constrain us to obey the law and accept certain obligations to pay taxes or serve in the army in times of war. We are not quite as 'free' as that grand narrative implies.

TIP: Look out for the 'grand narratives' in aspects of life that you are interested in, and test how close they are to the truth. For example:

Are estate agents dishonest?

Are business owners simply seeking to maximise their profits?

Are lawyers corrupt?

Do all professional footballers cheat?

If you are an estate agent, business person, lawyer or footballer you are sure to have an opinion. And if you are not you will be familiar with these common views about these professions.

'Lifescripting' is a particular form of storytelling which contains *your* design for life. Everybody does some lifescripting to varying degrees but the skilled lifescripter takes the process much more seriously and, as a result, has much more success. If you want to make a success of your life, start writing the script now.

Most people make plans, but they do not often do it consciously, nor do they do it with a sufficiently long term view. You should make the view as long term as you can. Even plan for your old age and death. This should not be seen as depressing. In fact, you should see it as quite the opposite. You must always be looking forward in writing a script and the furthest forward you can look is to your old age and death. But don't you want to have the best old age and death that you could possibly arrange? Well, the ability to start to do that is in your own hands now!

You have to see life as a play in which you are the writer, but also one of the main characters. You are writing your own script and setting the scene. Other characters will be obliged to do things in response to your character and your script. Have your character do things that 'make' the others do particular things. Whatever makes for a good play, can make for a good life. Each character has a profile. Your character has to mould something to the other characters' personality. Being one of the players is incidental. Being the writer is much more important. All the previous elements of this book can help design your character's profile and how it relates to the 'others' in the play.

Actors cannot act without a script if they are to achieve a desired and specific outcome. Decide the main goals of your performance. When writing your script remember that the 'voice' of self-improvement (of pulling yourself together) is calm and encouraging without being aggressive. It is welcoming and embracing. It advises without admonishing. Self-improvement adopts a language of the possible, conveying a sense of challenge with optimism about outcomes.

The conductor Herbet von Karajan recollected how he prepared for horse jumping. He used to lie awake at night worrying about how he would lift his horse, this huge creature, over the jump. Then he realised that all he had to do was get the horse in the right position and it would lift itself. He then applied the same with the orchestras he led. He just had to get them in the right position and they would 'lift themselves'.

When planning your script you have to begin by outlining the central character – you. Here's an example of the character outline for my life script.

My 'play' is entitled: **The Gentle Way**
(...and having read so far into this book you will realise the fundamental reasons for my character being scripted the way it is.)

Ron is a person who...
takes time to walk out for coffee in the morning;
when catching a plane, takes the slow and more pleasant route to the airport;
if taking a train catches the one best suited, leaving at the right time and stopping if necessary;
wherever he goes takes a notebook and/or sketchbook – not just a digital camera;
when working has his drawing board, easel, or musical instrument nearby;
either doesn't have a TV or radio or has strict rules for their use;
does not feel obliged to answer e-mails immediately;
does not surf the Web mindlessly to avoid being distracted by the possibilities – he 'searches' with a goal in mind.

His character is to be a *marchand du bonheur* (a purveyor of happiness) and his underlying relationship with people asks:
What can I do for you?

That gives you some insight into my lifescript. It certainly does not have to be yours.
NOW WRITE YOUR OWN CHARACTER OUTLINE.

One slight word of caution: in constructing your lifescript, take care not to make too many assumptions about the characters you will be interacting with. Be prepared for the possibility that their scripting is being written by someone else – such as themselves: don't ever assume that a van driver hasn't got a degree in Eastern Philosophy.

WAY 47 Success stories

In scripting your own life it can be useful to look at other people's successes. What did they seek and how did they get there? You might not wish to simply emulate them but there may be some lessons to be learned from their experience.

In fact, we all need to keep on learning throughout life. Many years ago I went to a workshop led by Alan Tuckett, who was the Director of the UK National Institute of Adult and Continuing Education. The event was for tutors in adult education and Alan asked which of them were actually attending a course of formal education themselves – the answer was no one. He then asked if anyone was actually 'learning something new' on an informal basis – again no one. (Actually there was one hand raised on both occasions – mine of course! I was on a Master's course and teaching myself classical guitar.) But his point was clear: how could these professionals understand their students if they were not also learning something new themselves? A successful adult educator should also be a learner. But really that applies to all of us – if we stop learning, we stop everything.

There is no one way to achieve success in personal development. There is only *your* way and my way. Each of us must write our own script for our lives (Markham 1993). Each script contains our own past, present and future. There are common elements, to be sure, and these are what I have presented to you in this book. Now you must go out and write your own and, more importantly, live it.

The stories which are told and which we tell about personal development must compete with other stories from a range of other sources. Some stories hold supremacy over the arena in which we each strive to make sense of our lives. As we do this we are sure to '… understand and misunderstand each other, co-operate and compete, join hands and part company, find happiness or disaster' (Cupitt 1991: 21).

When I coached tennis I came across a family who all played tennis apart from one member. She felt quite left out when the family went off to play a game. She had tried hard but she couldn't even hit the ball. All the family had tried to help her, with little success. You will recall Tim Gallwey's inner game from Way 25 where he suggests that what is getting in the way are beliefs that one cannot succeed: she told herself she was the person in the family who couldn't play the game, and she believed that story about herself. In fact her belief that she couldn't hit the ball was so strong that all coaching instructions failed. The instruction to 'Keep your eye on the ball' is not strong enough to counter the message she told herself: 'I am someone who is bound to miss.' What Gallwey suggests is we need to keep the mind focused on simple things and to speak them out loud. So, as he advised, I got her to say 'bounce' when she saw the ball hit the ground and 'hit' when it was hit by her racquet and again when I hit it. 'Bounce – hit, bounce – hit.' And she had to speak it out loud. Within ten minutes she was hitting the ball and she only missed when she forgot to speak the words out loud. I have used this technique successfully with many other people. More importantly, you can do it with other activities in life. Gallwey has suggested it for golf and music, amongst other activities.

The inner game is a form of mindfulness that has recently become quite popular. It keeps us focused on the task in hand and prevents the doubting voice emerging and undermining our success goals. In this way we can ensure our script concentrates on our successes.

TIP: Keep your personal instructions simple and from time to time speak them out loud even if you are on your own.

WAY 48 Manage your metaphors

Our lifescript will contain many different kinds of metaphors. The story of our life is managed through the metaphors we choose. A metaphor is merely an implied comparison and often used as a rhetorical device to persuade us to view a situation in a certain way. For example, people sometimes describe the ups and downs they are feeling in a stressful situation as a 'roller coaster of emotions'; they are not literally on a roller coaster, even though the feelings of rapid ups and downs can be compared to that. Most metaphors are hidden and taken for granted so we forget that they are not literal. They are only analogies for the experience we are having. But often the metaphors we choose can affect how we have the experience.

Thus Florence Scovel-Shinn exhorted us to see life not as a battle but as a 'game' (1925: 7). The problem is that if we see it as a battle we assume there must be winners and losers in the contest. But if we see it as a game it becomes less serious, we can look for the 'rules' of the game and techniques for 'playing' it. Play has a much gentler effect on the mind and body than does confrontation, and the metaphor produces a certain image at a quite subconscious level. In the racquet sports I used to play I succeeded more when I immersed myself in the 'game' rather than when I simply wanted to 'defeat' my opponent.

Explore what your metaphor for life is.

Do you have more than one metaphor?

Has it/have they changed as a result of reading this book?

Does it/do they need to change further?

I used to have a recurring dream that I was supposed to be joining my team for a game of football. But I couldn't find the field where the game was going on. I kept finding myself in the wrong 'field'. In some respects this was a wonderful parallel for my professional life. I do have diverse interests. I could never quite find my 'field' and I do suspect it is a problem for all social scientists; you do have to be a bit interested in everything. However, it does not help meet the demands of modern professional life which require a much more precise focus.

But my dream was clearly telling me that I needed to find the right field. Actually that search led me to study hypnosis and learn to apply it clinically. And that has led to this book, after all. Perhaps my somewhat circuitous route can have a direct benefit to you, since I have been passing on some of my 'trials and errors'. Drawing on another metaphor: take care not to 'muddy the water' – keep it clean, clear and flowing.

WAY 49 Holistic narratives

As you construct your narrative strive to incorporate all the elements that so far have had some resonance for you. Plan your 'Journey of Life'. Sometimes when starting out on a trip we see things in a different light. By breaking the routines we look afresh at the familiar. Whatever the trip, it is best to plan it so that you know where you are going, or at least roughly the direction in which you wish to head.

I used to write career plans all the time. Concept maps, lists, flow diagrams with obstacles to overcome and achievements to aim at: write the book, write some articles, do some research, get the PhD, get a better job, earn more money, start a clinic, run workshops, advertise more and so on. All of these goals had to fit within my overall plan to form my 'holistic narrative'.

One device for steering your journey is to write a 'happy list': a list of the things that you wish to do that you believe will make you happy. Here's an example of my happy list, written in 2003.

'I would be happy if...

1) I had written some books.

2) I was respected as an independent scholar and invited to speak to groups in business, academia, health, etc.

3) I had a network of interested contacts on whom I could draw, and who could draw upon me, for information, ideas and opportunities.

4) I could spend most of my time writing and reading, and some of my time doing therapy and occasionally giving talks and/or workshops.

5) I was living in an environmentally friendly house in a quiet rural area with friendly, unintrusive neighbours and in a warm climate. But I had a second small apartment in an interesting city with more opportunities for varied cultural engagement when I needed it.

6) I was earning good money from books, therapy and lecture tours on human well-being.'

I am not quite there yet, but I have accomplished much of this and I certainly know what it is I am aiming at.

TIP: Now do your happy list.

Start with 'I would be happy if...'

And remember to leave room for compromise. If we are too rigid, too dogmatic, we can miss out on opportunities. Include 'flexibility' as one of your treasured characteristics. I believe that you *can* have everything you desire if moderation remains your key principle. 'Everything in moderation' is a wise motto. By having everything in moderation nothing in excess can damage anything of what you have. And this could happen globally if we let it. There is enough of everything to go round. We could all live healthily in an environment that was clean and fresh and cultured – and we could do this in towns, cities, countryside and by the sea or in the mountains. We can all be spiritually and materially wealthy. These are not contradictory goals.

Self-help and personal development activities are not simply part of some vague and supposedly fashionable New Age movement. The links between mind and spirit, body and universe are becoming increasingly evident across many orthodox spheres. Feng shui, shamanism, divination, self-healing, past lives and prophecies are all about organising our lives for the best. They entail an awareness of the need to gain control of the mind to ensure control over the body; and the need for individuals to take responsibility for themselves. Even astrology is less fatalistic than many suppose, concentrating as it does upon the power of the individual will within the constraints of the cosmos. Biographical outcomes are by no means inevitably produced by planetary conjunction. Decision-making and risk-taking are simply seen as better informed when taken in the light of the influence of 'the stars'.

Scripts would be incomplete without some catchphrases or mantras that you can repeat to yourself. There have been many throughout this book, but if there is a single one that serves the purpose of supporting your life script it would be:

'Think it through!'

Do not act unthinkingly or without thought for the consequences of your actions for yourself and to others. Of course you cannot do that all the time, but even if you cultivate habits that do not require you to think too much then, before it becomes a habit, decide if you want it to be! Nothing happened yesterday, and nothing will happen tomorrow; everything happens now.

'There is only one success... to be able to spend your life in your own way...'
Christopher Morley

SOME THOUGHTS ON CLOSING

'The art of life lies in a constant readjustment to our surroundings.'
Okakura Kakuzo

It may sound as if I have been describing perfection throughout this book. But perfection can only be something to take aim at. The trick is to avoid the frustration that goes with apparently not achieving it. You don't have to be perfect. You can't be because perfection is a 'moving target'. Life, society, our environment are all constantly changing. So, perfection is a target to set your sights on to help you make judgements about where you are currently positioned in relation to your idea of perfection. It helps you appreciate what you have achieved, what you still wish to achieve and how you wish to relate to the important others in your life on your way to those achievements.

Even if you are not able to do all of the things I have suggested here, be happy to attempt some of them. Much of life is a compromise and just because you can't do everything, it does not mean you should do nothing.

More importantly, do remember that in re-educating your mind and your body there are consequences for which you should be prepared. The new practices suggested here will be having a 'detoxifying' effect and you will notice these creating changes in your mind and your body. Expect some discomfort arising from the mental and physical changes you are going through. Changes to diet, to physical exercise and to mental processing are all designed to eliminate toxins – those things that obstructed your move forward. Eliminating toxins is always uncomfortable but once they are gone the change you experience is wonderful.

You may also be challenged by the thought that you are going through a learning process and you may be concerned about how you will remember everything I have suggested. So try the following:

> **TIP:** There are really two vital principles to effective learning:
>
> 1) Spread out your study of this topic and return to it periodically – don't try to learn and remember it all at once.
>
> 2) Link or interweave these learning points to other events, tasks and topics in your life.
>
> (see Brown, Roediger and McDaniel 2014 for the evidence about how this learning works).

You can go back to different sections in the book from time to time to try out the exercises and/or remind yourself of some essential technique. Also pick up other books in the *49 Ways* series that can take each of these chapters further. And note how I have shown how the larger project of pulling yourself together can be mirrored in smaller projects – such as learning to play a musical instrument, or doing the shopping, decorating the house or gardening. Seeking well-being is about harmony in both your internal and external environment. That harmony is then mirrored in the health of your mind and your body.

There are aspects to what I am suggesting to you here that are quite hard to achieve. For example, it is quite hard to recognise a 'sunk fund' when it was originally a cherished goal. And then it is even harder to stop heading for it and to redefine your goals, your dreams and your ways of getting there. But if you are walking towards something and, for whatever reason, you become aware that it is no longer the dream you thought, it then becomes quite hard to let go of it and find another goal. But there is nothing 'wrong' in that. In fact it is essential. And we often stick to a project because of what 'others' may think about us. They say: 'But I thought you wanted to...' So what! What they think or think you thought is irrelevant to you finding your dream and changing it if you wish to.

Change is never comfortable but that doesn't mean you shouldn't do it. My wife and I now live in France. It was our dream but now we have another and it might mean moving elsewhere – so why not?

Don't wait for your ship to come in – swim out to it.

Use your dreams. Accept synchronicity. Be flexible to keep your sight on that moving target. Follow your path and look out for the signposts that will emerge. One aim of this book has been to show that narrative is powerful. It is through the words we use, the stories we tell ourselves, that connections are made between mind, body and society. Looking at the stories that a community allows or encourages its members to tell themselves reveals a great deal about that community's values and destination. It is up to each individual to decide how to participate in that process and how to remedy its more damaging aspects.

Paungger and Poppe (2013) remind us of the fable of a pig that comes to a river and sees a magnificent compost heap on the other side with all the sorts of tasty things that pigs like to eat. As he thinks out loud: 'I wonder if the water is shallow enough for me to wade across?' a mole emerges and says: 'I think it is, give it a try.' The pig jumps in and soon discovers it is far too deep and only just manages to scramble back to the bank and crawl ashore.

He complains to the mole who replies: 'That's funny, the water only comes up to the breast of the ducks I have seen there.' What works for one individual does not necessarily work for all.

By designing your life in the ways suggested and modified by you, you will be living a more authentic life. Living life authentically means helping your own ego to find the best possible path to freedom. It means having the courage to weather the initial protests of those who would, for their own reasons, have you live only the same sort of life as they have allowed themselves to live. For the most part they have not chosen their lives, they have lacked the courage to make the choices necessary for change and they are often afraid of those with the courage to allow themselves to be different.

Life is about compassion, love and responsibility, both for oneself and for others. The purpose of life is to find for yourself the best way to live. Many accomplished writers and therapists have suggested what life is all about: for Victor Frankl it is a search for meaning, for Erich Fromm 'love' is the ultimate need and desire of all human beings. Each of us has to find the best way for ourselves but we cannot do that alone since most lives have to be lived in the light of others. We learn that 'best way' from others and we, in turn, can help others to find their 'best way'. I hope that this book has played some little part in how you come to live your life for the best. Of course there are more than 49 ways. This is not the end. This is a start.

WHERE DO I GO FROM HERE?

What you read and do next depends very much on the particular angle that you need to take for your 'project'. These are other useful sources to help you think through gaining control of your life. From my experience I suggest the following routes to further discovery (full book information is in the reference list):

If you are interested in what might be thought of as a cosmological or even an astrological view of health then look at Paungger and Poppe's book *Moon Time*.

If you are prepared for a more meditative and Socratic examination of your relationships then try following Byron Katie's *The Work* (see www.thework.com).

If you need something spiritual or something that tries to explore our relationship with the divine then look at *Neale Donald Walsch's Conversations with God* or even consider following the *Course in Miracles* (see www.nealedonaldwalsch.com; www.acim.org).

An overarching and accessible perspective that is philosophically influenced can be found in Alain de Boton's writings and his School of Life (www.theschooloflife.com).

If you need to look at the evidence beyond more orthodox sources of health information then consider *What Doctors Don't Tell You* (www.wddty.com).

If you are interested in the links between the physical and the spiritual that are examined with scientific rigour, have a look at the Scientific and Medical Network (www.scimednet.org) and also the work of Fritjof Capra.

Phil McGraw's books help with both relationships and examination of your self.

Read *Resurgence and Ecologist* for a connection between the spiritual and the environmental.

To read more about the incentives that influence our decisions look at the series of 'freakonomics' books by Dubner and Levitt. Their work on behavioural economics supplements the 'nudge' work mentioned earlier (see www.freakonomics.com/about).

Often these sources cross-reference each other but they can also lead you on to other useful sources of direct relevance to your needs. Remember: do the research.

© freepik.com

FURTHER READING/REFERENCES

Alcoe, J. and Gajewski, E. (2013) *49 Ways to Think Yourself Well* Step Beach Press: Brighton

Anderson, K. (1999) *The Coincidence File*, London: Cassell Illustrated

Batmanghelidj, F. (2000) *Your Body's Many Cries for Water*, Norwich: Tagman Press

Bellamy, A. (2015) *49 Ways to Move Yourself Well* Step Beach Press: Brighton

Blakeslee, T.R. (1997) *The Attitude Factor*, London: Thorsons

Bode, R. (1993) *First You Have To Row a Little Boat (Reflections on Life and Living)*, New York: Warner Books. [An easy to read book that uses sailing as an allegory for dealing with life. You learn to sail as you learn how to make choices and deal with obstacles in life.]

Brown, P.C., Roediger, H.L., and McDaniel, M.A. (2014) *Make It Stick: The Science of Successful Learning*, Harvard: Harvard University Press

Cain, S. (2012) *Quiet: The Power of Introverts in a World That Can't Stop Talking*, London: Penguin Books

Cameron, J. (1994) *The Artist's Way*, London: Pan Books

Campbell, D. (1991) *Music: Physician for Times to Come*, Wheaton: Quest Books

Campbell, D. (1997) *The Mozart Effect*, London: HarperCollins

Canfield, J. and Hansen, M.V. (1993) *Chicken Soup for the Soul*, London: Random House

Capra, F. (1983) *The Turning Point: Science, Society and the Rising Culture*, London: Fontana

Capra, F. (2014) *The Systems View of Life: A Unifying Vision*, Cambridge: Cambridge University Press

Carnegie, D. (1994) *How to Win Friends and Influence People*, London: Chancellor Press (first published 1936). [One of the original personal development books. Based on Carnegie's evening classes – which grew in popularity so that he became one of the most famous adult educators. This contains inspirational stories, anecdotes, quotations and practical suggestions for self-development. This and all of his books are an easy read and quite inspirational.]

Carter, F. (2015) *49 Ways to Sexual Well-being* Step Beach Press: Brighton

Castaneda, C. (1970) *The Teachings of Don Juan*, Harmondsworth: Penguin

Chopra, D. (1996) *Creating Health (How to Wake up the Body's Intelligence)*, London: Thorsons (first published 1987)

Chopra, D. (1996) *The Seven Spiritual Laws of Success*, London: Bantam

Coué, E. (1960) *Better and Better Every Day* London: George Allen & Unwin [Two classic texts on the healing power of the mind]

Covey, S.R. (1994) *The Seven Habits of Highly Effective People*, London: Simon & Schuster

Cousins, N. (1979) *Anatomy of an Illness As Perceived by the Patient*, New York: Norton

Crawley, J. (1996) *The Biorhythm Book*, London: Eddison Sadd

Csikszentmihalyi, M. (1996) *Creativity: Flow and the Psychology of Discovery and Invention*, New York: HarperCollins

Csikszentmihalyi, M. (1997) *Finding Flow: The Psychology of Engagement with Everyday Life*, New York: Basic Books

Cupitt, D. (1991) *What is a Story?* London: SCM Press

Day, L. (1996) *Practical Intuition,* http://www.practicalintuition.com London: Vermillion

Diamond, H. and Diamond, M. (1985) *Fit For Life*, London: Bantam Books

Dossey, L. (1991) *Healing Breakthroughs: How Attitudes and Beliefs Can Affect Your Health*, London: Piatkus

Dossey, L. (1993) *Healing Words: The Power of Prayer and the Practice of Medicine*, San Francisco: HarperCollins

Ford, A. (1998) *Hot Chocolate for the Mystical Soul*, London: Thorsons

Foundation for Inner Peace (1996) *A Course in Miracles*, Harmondsworth: Penguin (first published 1975)

Franklin, B. (1995) *The Means and Manner of Obtaining Virtue*, Harmondsworth: Penguin (first published 1757)

Gallwey, W.T. (1975) *The Inner Game of Tennis*, London: Jonathan Cape

Gardner, H. (2004) *Changing Minds*, Boston: Harvard Business School Press

Gawain, S. (1995) *Creative Visualization*, Novato: New World Library

Gawain, S. (1997) T*he Four Levels of Healing*, Enfield: Eden Grove

Godefroy, C.H. and Clark, J. (1989) *The Complete Time Management System,* London: Piatkus

Grant, D. and Joice, J. (1984) *Food Combining for Health – A New Look at the Hay System*, London: Thorsons

Gray, J. (1993) *Men Are From Mars, Women Are From Venus*, London: Thorsons

Gray, J. (1997) *Mars And Venus On A Date (5 Steps to Success in Love and Romance)*, London: Random House

Green, B. with Gallwey, W.T. (1986) *The Inner Game of Music*, New York: Macmillan

Gros, F. (2014) *A Philosophy of Walking*, New York: Verso

Haden Elgin, S. (1989) *Success with the Gentle Art of Verbal Self-Defense,* New Jersey: Prentice Hall

Hall, N.R.S., Altman, F. and Blumenthal, S.J. (eds.) (1996) *Mind-Body Interactions and Disease and Psychoneuroimmunological Aspects of Health and Disease*, Orlando: Health Dateline Press

Hand, D.J. (2014) *The Improbability Principle: Why Coincidences, Miracles, and Rare Events Happen Every Day*, London: Scientific American

Hay, L.L. (1984) *You Can Heal Your Life*, Santa Monica: Hay House

Hayward, S. (1987) *You Have a Purpose – Begin it Now*, Avalon: In-Tune Books

Heelas, P. (1996) *The New Age Movement (The Celebration of the Self and the Sacralization of Modernity)*, Oxford: Blackwell

Helgoe, L. (2013) *Introvert Power*, Illinois: Sourcebooks

Helmstetter, S. (1986) *What to Say When You Talk to Yourself*, London: Thorsons

Holder, J, (2013) *49 Ways to Write Yourself Well* Step Beach Press: Brighton

Jackson Brown, H. (1993) *Life's Little Instruction Book*, London: Thorsons

Jahn, R.G. and Dunne, B.J. (1987) *Margins of Reality: The Role of Consciousness in the Physical World*, New York-San Diego: Harcourt Brace Jovanovich

Jahn, R.G. (1996) 'Information, Consciousness, and Health.' *Alternative Therapies in Health and Medicine*, 2(3): 32–38 (1996)

James, W. (1897) *The Will to Believe*, New York: Longman & Co.

Jampolsky, G. (1983) *Teach Only Love*, New York: Bantane

Jeffers, S. (1987) *Feel the Fear and Do It Anyway*, London: Rider

Josselson, R. and Lieblich, A. (eds.) (1993) *The Narrative Study of Lives*, Vol.1, London: Sage

Kakuzo, O. (1956) *The Book of Tea*, Tokyo: Charles E Tuttle Company

Kohn, A. (1990) *The Brighter Side of Human Nature: Altruism and Empathy in Everyday Life*, New York: Basic Books.

Le Tissier, J. (1992) *Food Combining for Vegetarians*, London: Thorsons

Liberman, J. (1995) T*ake off Your Glasses and See*, London: Thorsons

Lovett, M.A. (2011) *The Clutter Book: When You Can't Let Go*, Portus Publishing

Lyotard, J-F. (1984) *The Post Modern Condition*, Minneapolis: University of Minnesota Press

McGraw, P.C. (1999) *Life Strategies: Doing what works, Doing what matters*, New York: Hyperion

McGraw, P.C. (2000) *Relationship Rescue: A seven-step strategy for reconnecting with your partner*, New York: Hyperion

McGraw, P.C. (2001) *Self Matters: Creating Your Life From the Inside Out*, London: Simon and Schuster

05/15 TS

Mander, J. (1992) *In the Absence of the Sacred*, San Francisco: Sierra Club Books

Markham, U. (1993) *Life Scripts*, Shaftesbury: Element Books

Martin, P. (1997) *The Sickening Mind: Brain, Behaviour, Immunity and Disease*, London: HarperCollins

Matthews, A. (1988) *Being Happy (A Handbook to Greater Confidence and Security)*, Singapore: Media Masters

Miller, D.P. (1997) *The Complete Story of The Course*, London: Rider Books

Moore, T. (1996) *The Re-Enchantment of Everyday Life*, London: Hodder & Stoughton

Paungger, J. and Poppe, T. (1995) *Moon Time*, Saffron Walden: The CW Daniel Company Ltd.

Paungger, J. and Poppe, T. (2013) *The Power of Timing: Living in Harmony with Natural and Lunar Rhythms*, New York: Wisdom Keeper Books

Person, E.S. (1995) *The Force of Fantasy: Its Power to Transform Our Lives*, London: HarperCollins

Phillips, D.P., Ruth, T.E. and Wagner, L.M. (1994) 'Birth Signs, Death Signs', Harvard Mental Health Letter, May, 10(11)

Postman. N. (1982) *The Disappearance of Childhood*, New York: Delacorte Press

Postman, N. (1986) *Amusing Ourselves to Death: Public Discourse in the Age of Show Business*, London: Heinemann

Redfield, J. (1994) *The Celestine Prophecy (An Adventure)*, London: Bantam

Reissmann, C.K. (1993) *Narrative Analysis*, Newbury Park: Sage.

Reynolds, D.K. (1991) *Thirsty Swimming in the Lake (Essentials of Constructive Living)*, New York: Quill – William Morrow (www.constructiveliving.org/index.html)

Robbins, A. (1988) *Unlimited Power (The New Science of Personal Achievement)*, London: Simon & Schuster

Robbins, A. (1994) *Giant Steps: Small Changes to Make a Big Difference – 365 Daily Lessons in Self-Mastery*, New York: Simon & Schuster

Samways, L. (1997) *The 12 Secrets of Health & Happiness*, Harmondsworth: Penguin

Satir, V. (1976) *Making Contact*, Berkeley CA: Celestial Arts

Satir, V. (1972) *Peoplemaking*, Palo Alto: Science and Behavior Books

Scott Peck, M. (1978) *The Road Less Travelled*, London: Rider

Scovel-Shinn, F. (1925) *The Game of Life and How to Play It*, Romford: L.N. Fowler & Co. Ltd (39th Edition 1991)

Sheldrake, R. (2011) *Dogs That Know When Their Owners are Coming Home and Other Unexplained Powers of Animals* (2nd Edition) New York: Three Rivers Press

Sheldrake, R. (2014) 'Telepathy in Connection with Telephone Calls, Text Messages and Emails', *Journal of International Society of Life Information Science*, Vol 32. No.1

Smiles, S. (1958) *Self-Help* (With a centenary introduction by Professor Asa Briggs), London: John Murray

Smiles, S. (1866) *Self-Help: With illustrations of character and conduct*, London: John Murray

Smith, R. (1998) *Lessons From the Dying*, Somerville, MA: Wisdom Publications

Stapleton, R.W. and Waller, T. (1997) *The Karma Bear*, Devizes: Selecta Books

Thaler, R.H. and Sunstein, C.R. (2009) *Nudge: Improving Decisions About Health, Wealth and Happiness*, London: Penguin Books

Thoreau, H.D. (1996) *Walden*, Cologne: Konemann (first published 1854)

Time Magazine, (29/11/76)

Tolle, E. (1997) *The Power of Now*, Vancouver: Amaste Publishing

Waters, M. (1996) *The Element Dictionary of Personal Development*, Shaftesbury: Element Press

Watts, M. (2012) *49 Ways to Eat Yourself Well* Step Beach Press: Brighton

Wilson, P. (1996) *The Little Book of Calm*, Harmondsworth: Penguin